Built For More

The Elevated Man Project

CADE BROWN

ISBN: 9781764771924

DEDICATION

To my two Pops, Victor Lewis Johnston and John Patrick O'Connor.

Two men who shaped my life in different ways, each leaving lessons, values, and memories that continue to guide me long after the moments themselves have passed. Thank you for your love, your sacrifices, your wisdom, and the example you set. Much of the man I am today was built upon the foundations you helped create. I carry your lessons with me every day, and I hope this book honours the legacy of the men you were.

To my son, Marinko.

You remind me daily that strength and kindness can coexist, that courage often looks like vulnerability, and that our differences are not flaws to overcome but gifts to embrace. My greatest hope is that when you grow into a man, you never question your worth, your value, or your place in this world. You were never broken. You were always enough.

And finally, this book is dedicated to all the men we have lost to suicide. The fathers. The sons. The brothers. The husbands. The mates. The men who carried burdens they believed they had to carry alone. The men who convinced themselves that the world would be better without them. It wouldn't have been. Your absence is felt. Your lives mattered. Your stories mattered. You mattered.

May we continue building a world where men feel safe enough to speak, strong enough to ask for help, and supported enough to know they never have to walk through darkness alone.

And to every man reading this who is still here, still fighting, still carrying on despite the weight on his shoulders:

This book is for you too. Keep going, the world needs you.

CONTENTS

ACKNOWLEDGEMENTS

No man becomes who he is alone.

One of the greatest lies many men believe is that strength means independence. That somehow we are supposed to carry every burden by ourselves, figure everything out on our own, and walk through life without needing help from anyone.

The truth is very different.

Every man who has ever become something meaningful was helped by other people along the way.

This book is no exception.

First and foremost, to my wife, Jana.

Thank you for twenty years of love, patience, support, and partnership.

You have stood beside me through some of the highest highs and lowest lows of my life. You have celebrated my victories, challenged me when I needed it, and supported me when I struggled to support myself.

Thank you for believing in me, even during the times I struggled to believe in myself.

I love you more than words can adequately express.

To my son, Marinko.

You have been one of my greatest teachers.

Every day you remind me what truly matters. Your courage, your curiosity, your honesty, and your unique way of seeing the world have challenged me to become a better father, and a better man.

You are one of the reasons this book exists.

I hope one day when you read these pages, you will understand how deeply loved you are and how proud I am to be your dad.

To my friend Leon Wilken.

Thank you for introducing me to the Alpha Code and, in many ways, helping me begin a journey that changed the trajectory of my life. You have consistently demonstrated what masculine leadership, courage, resilience, and purpose look like in practice. Thank you for your friendship, your guidance, and your example.

Your documentary, When The Mountains Talk, continues to inspire men to embrace challenge, growth, and self-discovery. The lessons within it have touched countless lives, including my own. If you're serious about becoming a better man, I highly encourage you to watch it on YouTube.

https://www.youtube.com/watch?v=uAPew-IY8oY

To my friend Lucas Cope.

Thank you for your friendship, loyalty, and example.

As a fellow Brazilian Jiu-Jitsu Black Belt and long-serving police officer, you have spent your life serving others while quietly embodying the values of discipline, humility, courage, and integrity.

You lead through action rather than words, and our community is better because of it.

To my friend Clay Greenbank.

Thank you for your friendship, honesty, and example over the years.

You have shown me the profound impact a father can have on a son's life. Through your leadership, guidance, and presence, you've raised a strong, capable, respectful young man in Jordon. Watching the relationship between you and your son has been a powerful reminder that fatherhood is one of the greatest forms of leadership a man can undertake.

The example you've set, both as a man and as a father, has reinforced my belief that the greatest legacy we leave is not what we achieve, but who we help shape. Thank you for leading by example and for demonstrating what character, and fatherhood look like when lived with purpose.

To Justin Dulihanty, founder of the Men's Development Academy.

Thank you for creating a movement that has helped thousands of men reclaim responsibility, purpose, and self-respect.

Your commitment to helping men become stronger leaders, husbands, fathers, and human beings has had a profound impact on my life and on the lives of countless others.

The ripple effect of your work will be felt for generations.

To my Alpha Coach, Kalan Hall.

Thank you for challenging me when I needed challenging and supporting me when I needed support. You had the courage to tell me what I needed to hear rather than what I wanted to hear.

Your guidance, accountability, and belief in my potential helped me navigate some of the most important transformations of my life. Many of the lessons contained within these pages were forged through conversations, reflections, and breakthroughs we shared together.

To the men of the Alpha Code and the Men's Development Academy.

Thank you for your honesty, vulnerability, courage, and brotherhood.

In a world where many men suffer in silence, you created a space where men could speak openly, challenge one another, grow together, and become stronger.

The lessons I learned from being surrounded by men committed to growth changed my life.

To every mentor, coach, teacher, friend, and brother who has walked beside me throughout this journey. Thank you.

Every conversation mattered. Every lesson mattered. Every challenge mattered. Every piece of wisdom contributed to the man writing these words today.

And finally, to every man reading this book.

Thank you for trusting me enough to take this journey with you.

I know what it's like to feel disconnected.

To feel like you're carrying the weight of the world on your shoulders.

I know what it's like to question your worth, your direction, and your place in the world.

I also know what is possible when a man chooses to take responsibility for his life.

This book was written for you.

My hope is that somewhere within these pages you find a lesson, an insight, a challenge, or a perspective that helps you reconnect with the man you were always capable of becoming.

The world needs strong men. Not perfect men. Strong men.

Men with integrity. Men with courage. Men with character. Men willing to lead themselves and serve others.

Thank you for being one of them.

INTRODUCTION

Welcome To The Elevated Man Project

If you're holding this book, there's a good chance something in your life isn't working.

Maybe your relationship is struggling.

Maybe you're exhausted from carrying everyone else's problems.

Maybe you've achieved success but still feel empty.

Maybe you're stuck in a cycle of self-doubt, people-pleasing, procrastination, or emotional exhaustion.

Or maybe you've simply reached a point where you're tired of being the man you've become and know you're capable of more.

Whatever brought you here, I want you to know something.

You're not alone.

And you're not broken.

In fact, one of the biggest lies modern men have been taught is that something is wrong with them.

That they're not confident enough.

Not successful enough.

Not masculine enough.

Not disciplined enough.

Not worthy enough.

So they spend years trying to fix themselves.

Reading books.

Listening to podcasts.

Watching videos.

Attending seminars.

Searching for answers.

I know because I was one of them.

For years, I thought the solution was becoming more.

More successful.

More capable.

More money.

More discipline.

More motivation.

More status.

More approval.

More validation.

But underneath all those pursuits is often something much deeper.

A man who has forgotten who he is.

I know because I was that man.

This book exists because I became that man.

And nearly lost everything because of it.

Why I Wrote This Book

I didn't write this book because I'm perfect.

Far from it.

I didn't write it because I've figured everything out.

I haven't.

I wrote it because I've lived what these pages contain.

I've lived the people-pleasing.

The approval addiction.

The self-abandonment.

The emotional suppression.

The fear.

The shame.

The self-doubt.

The depression.

The confusion.

And I've also lived the transformation.

I've experienced what happens when a man stops trying to earn his worth and starts recognising it.

I've experienced what happens when he develops boundaries.

Learns emotional intelligence.

Confronts his fears.

Builds self-respect.

Lives by a code.

Leads himself.

I wrote this book because I know there are men who desperately need to hear what nobody ever told them.

You don't need to become someone else.

You need to come home to yourself.

The Promise Of This Book

I cannot promise that this book will make your life easy.

Life isn't easy.

I cannot promise that you'll never experience fear.

You will.

I cannot promise that you'll never experience pain.

You will.

What I can promise is this.

If you genuinely apply what you learn in these pages:

You will develop greater confidence.

Not performative confidence.

Real confidence.

The kind built on self-trust.

You will develop healthier boundaries.

Stronger relationships.

Greater emotional intelligence.

Improved self-respect.

More resilience.

More courage.

More clarity.

More purpose.

More peace.

Most importantly, you will begin building a relationship with yourself that no longer depends on external validation.

And that changes everything.

What Is The Elevated Man Project?

The Elevated Man Project is not another self-help program.

It's not a motivational slogan.

It's not about becoming an alpha male.

It's not about dominating people.

It's not about pretending to be tough.

It's not about status.

It's not about ego.

It's about becoming the man you are capable of becoming.

Nothing more.

Nothing less.

An Elevated Man understands his worth.

He takes responsibility.

He leads himself.

He tells the truth.

He honours his values.

He sets boundaries.

He processes emotions.

He loves deeply without losing himself.

He lives courageously.

He leaves people better than he found them.

He becomes an example worth following.

Not because he's perfect.

Because he's committed.

Committed to growth.

Committed to integrity.

Committed to becoming.

That is The Elevated Man Project.

And this book is your invitation into that journey.

Before We Begin

I need to warn you about something.

If you genuinely engage with this book, it will challenge you.

It will challenge your beliefs.

Your excuses.

Your habits.

Your stories.

Your identity.

There will be chapters that make you uncomfortable.

Good.

Growth lives there.

There will be moments where you recognise yourself in these pages.

Good.

Awareness is where transformation begins.

There will be moments where you want to put the book down.

Good.

That's usually a sign you've touched something important.

Because this isn't a book about becoming someone new.

It's a book about uncovering who you've always been underneath the conditioning, fear, approval-seeking, and self-doubt.

The man you're looking for is already there.

This journey is simply about meeting him.

So take a deep breath.

Turn the page.

And let's begin.

Welcome to The Elevated Man Project.

PART I

THE GREAT DISCONNECTION

How Good Men Lose Themselves

CHAPTER ONE

The Good Man Trap

When being a good man becomes a prison

I used to think being a good man was enough.

Actually, that's not true.

I thought being a good man would save me.

I thought if I worked hard enough, loved deeply enough, sacrificed enough, and put everyone else's needs before my own, life would eventually reward me.

I thought happiness was something you earned.

Respect was something you earned.

Love was something you earned.

Worthiness was something you earned.

The problem is that when your entire life becomes an attempt to earn your value, you're never allowed to stop proving it.

And that's a fucking exhausting way to live.

For most of my life, I wasn't consciously aware of this.

Like many men, I wore my self-sacrifice like a badge of honour.

I was loyal.

Dependable.

Protective.

Generous.

I loved my family fiercely.

I would do anything for the people I cared about.

And that's what made the trap so difficult to see.

Because nothing about it looked unhealthy.

From the outside, it looked admirable.

But there was a hidden cost.

The cost was me.

The Boy Who Learned Love Had Conditions

Nobody wakes up at thirty-five years old and decides to become a people-pleaser.

Nobody sits down one morning and says:

"You know what sounds like a great idea? Constantly ignoring my own needs while desperately seeking approval from everyone around me."

That would be ridiculous.

People-pleasing is learned.

It's an adaptation.

It's a survival strategy.

And like most survival strategies, it begins long before we're old enough to understand what we're doing.

As children, we have one primary objective.

Connection.

We need love.

We need safety.

We need acceptance.

We need to feel seen.

And children are incredibly resourceful.

If being quiet gets us love, we become quiet.

If being helpful gets us love, we become helpful.

If being responsible gets us love, we become responsible.

If taking care of everyone else's emotions gets us love, we become caretakers.

We learn who we need to become to receive the connection we desperately need.

The problem is that what helps us survive childhood often sabotages adulthood.

Somewhere along the way, many men unconsciously develop a belief that sounds something like this:

"My value comes from what I do for other people."

Not because anyone explicitly taught it to us.

Because life conditioned us into believing it.

And once that belief takes root, it quietly begins shaping everything.

Your relationships.

Your career.

Your decisions.

Your boundaries.

Your confidence.

Your identity.

Eventually you stop asking:

"What do I want?"

And start asking:

"What do they need?"

Over.

And over.

And over again.

Until one day you realise you've become a supporting character in your own life.

The Nice Guy Lie

Most Nice Guys are not actually nice.

That statement usually pisses people off.

Good.

Stay with me.

I'm not saying they're bad people.

I'm saying many of their behaviours are driven by fear rather than authenticity.

A genuinely kind man gives because it aligns with his values.

A Nice Guy often gives because he hopes to receive something in return.

Approval.

Validation.

Love.

Acceptance.

Security.

The exchange is usually unconscious.

He isn't manipulating anyone.

He genuinely believes he's being a good person.

But underneath the behaviour is often an invisible contract.

The contract says:

"If I give enough, they'll love me."

"If I sacrifice enough, they'll appreciate me."

"If I'm patient enough, they'll change."

"If I'm understanding enough, they'll respect me."

"If I'm good enough, I'll finally feel enough."

The problem?

Nobody else signed that contract.

So eventually resentment arrives.

Resentment is often the emotional receipt for expectations we never communicated.

Read that again.

Resentment is often the emotional receipt for expectations we never communicated.

Most Nice Guys don't struggle because they're too caring.

They struggle because they care for everyone except themselves.

When Love Becomes Self-Abandonment

One of the greatest strengths in my life has always been my love for my family.

My wife Jana is one of the most incredible human beings I've ever met.

I knew she was special from the moment I first saw her.

Twenty years later, she's still the love of my life.

But love creates a unique challenge for men like me.

Because when you love deeply, it's easy to start measuring your worth through the people you love.

I became incredibly invested in being a good husband.

A good father.

A good provider.

A good protector.

Again, these aren't bad goals.

They're admirable goals.

The problem came when those roles stopped being expressions of who I was and became the source of who I was.

That's a dangerous shift.

Because when your identity becomes dependent on your roles, you begin losing yourself inside them.

You stop asking:

"What kind of life do I want?"

And start asking:

"What do I need to do to keep everyone else happy?"

You avoid conflict.

You soften your opinions.

You tolerate things you shouldn't tolerate.

You suppress your needs.

You sacrifice your desires.

You convince yourself you're doing it for love.

Sometimes you are.

Sometimes you're doing it because you're terrified of what might happen if you don't.

There's a difference.

And that difference changes everything.

The Day Everything Nearly Ended

There was a time in my life when I didn't want to be here anymore.

Not because I didn't care about life.

But because the weight of it had become too heavy to carry.

From the outside everything looked fine.

But depression doesn't care about appearances.

Inside I was falling apart.

Depression is quiet.

It creeps in slowly, like fog rolling across a landscape.

At first you don't even realise it's happening.

You just feel a little more tired than usual.

A little less motivated.

A little more disconnected.

And then one day you wake up and the fog is everywhere.

You start questioning your worth.

Your value.

Your place in the world.

Your mind begins telling you stories.

Dangerous stories.

Stories that say:

"You're not enough."

"You're a burden."

"The world would be better without you."

And when those stories repeat long enough, they start to sound like truth.

For a long time I carried that weight in silence.

Like many people do.

Because somewhere along the way, many of us learned that struggling with mental health means we're weak.

That asking for help means we're failing.

So we push through.

We put on a brave face.

We keep performing the version of ourselves we think the world expects.

Depression has a way of stripping your identity away.

It takes every insecurity, every fear, every unresolved wound, and turns the volume up.

It convinces you that your value is conditional.

Eventually I reached a moment where the pain felt unbearable.

A moment where my mind convinced me that the only way to stop the suffering, was to stop existing.

And if you've ever found yourself in a dark place, you know exactly what I mean.

But here's the truth that people often miss about suicidal moments.

They're not usually about wanting to die.

They're about wanting the pain to stop.

There's an enormous difference.

I reached a moment where the pain became louder than the hope.

A moment where I made a decision that I can hardly believe now.

I tried to end my life.

What I remember next is difficult to describe.

There was nothing.

Just blackness.
No sound. No movement. No sense of time.
It was like everything had simply stopped.
And then something strange began to happen.
Through the darkness I started to see flashes of light.
Just brief bursts.
Light, then darkness again.
Light, then darkness again.
At first they were faint, almost like distant sparks.
But they kept coming.
Over and over again.
In rhythm.
A flash of light, then black.
Another flash, then black.

And slowly, somewhere in that darkness, my body began fighting its way back.
Those flashes of light weren't random.
They were the rhythm of my heart trying to start again.
They were the chest compressions of someone refusing to let me go.
Someone who found me.
Someone who stepped in at the exact moment my life was slipping away.
Someone I will always think of as an angel.

Because in that moment, when I had given up on myself, someone else hadn't.
They kept fighting for my life until my heart started beating again.
Until the darkness began to lift.
Until I was pulled back.
I had been given a second chance.
A chance I very nearly didn't have.
And that second chance changed the way I see everything.

It made me realise how powerful our minds can be, both in the way they can pull us down, and in the way they can help us rise again.

It made me realise that even when someone feels completely alone in their suffering, their life still matters.

More than they realise.

More than their mind may allow them to believe in that moment.

And it made me realise something else.

It was the realisation that if I ended my life, I would also end every possibility that still existed for it.

Every future moment.

Every chance to heal.

Every chance to become someone stronger.

Every chance to be present for the people I love.

Including a little boy who calls me Daddy.

The miracle wasn't simply that I survived.

The miracle was what surviving forced me to confront.

For the first time in my life, I had to ask myself a question I had spent decades avoiding.

Who am I when I'm not trying to earn my worth?

That question became the foundation of everything that followed.

The Real Problem

Most men think they have a confidence problem.

They don't.

Most men think they have a motivation problem.

They don't.

Most men think they need more discipline.

Sometimes they do.

But that's rarely the root issue.

The real issue is identity.

Because confidence is not built by forcing yourself to act confident.

Confidence is built when your actions align with who you know yourself to be.

The man who constantly seeks approval doesn't trust himself.

The man who constantly explains himself doesn't trust himself.

The man who constantly needs validation doesn't trust himself.

The issue isn't confidence.

The issue is self-trust.

And self-trust can never exist while you're abandoning yourself.

Every time you say yes when you mean no.

You weaken self-trust.

Every time you suppress your truth.

You weaken self-trust.

Every time you tolerate behaviour that violates your values.

You weaken self-trust.

Eventually your relationship with yourself becomes fractured.

And when you don't trust yourself, life feels unstable.

Not because the world is unstable.

Because your foundation is.

The Truth That Changed Everything

My biggest breakthrough wasn't learning how to be more confident.

It wasn't learning how to lead.

It wasn't learning how to set boundaries.

It wasn't learning how to communicate.

Those things mattered.

But they came later.

The breakthrough was realising that my worth wasn't something I needed to earn.

It already existed.

For years I had operated from a belief that sounded noble.

"I am valuable because I am needed."

The healthier belief is:

"I am valuable because I exist."

One belief creates exhaustion.

The other creates freedom.

One requires endless proving.

The other allows you to simply be.

One creates a Nice Guy.

The other creates an Elevated Man.

The Elevated Man doesn't stop caring.

He doesn't stop loving.

He doesn't stop serving.

He simply stops abandoning himself while doing it.

That's the difference.

And that difference changes everything.

The Elevated Man Challenge

For the next seven days, carry a notebook or use your phone.

Every time you notice yourself:

- Saying yes when you want to say no.
- Seeking approval before making a decision.
- Avoiding a difficult conversation.
- Apologising unnecessarily.
- Prioritising someone else's comfort over your truth.

Write it down.

Don't judge it.

Don't change it.

Just notice it.

Awareness always comes before transformation.

Because you cannot rebuild a man until you first identify where he's been abandoning himself.

And chances are, you've been doing it for far longer than you realise.

CHAPTER TWO

The Cost Of Being Needed

Why usefulness became your identity

There was a time in my life when being needed felt like love.

Actually, it felt better than love.

Love can be uncertain.

Love can be questioned.

Love can disappear.

But being needed?

Being needed feels concrete.

If people need you, they call you.

If people need you, they rely on you.

If people need you, they keep you around.

If people need you, you matter.

At least that's what I believed.

I didn't consciously think:

"My worth depends on being needed."

Nobody thinks that.

Instead, it shows up in the way you live.

You become the helper.

The fixer.

The rescuer.

The provider.

The emotional caretaker.

The dependable one.

The man everyone relies on.

And because society rewards those behaviours, nobody tells you there's a problem.

In fact, people praise you for it.

"You're such a great guy."

"You're always there for everyone."

"I don't know what we'd do without you."

Those compliments feel incredible.

Not because they're true.

Because they feed the addiction.

The addiction isn't helping.

The addiction is significance.

The addiction is feeling valuable.

The addiction is believing your existence matters because somebody depends on you.

And that addiction nearly cost me everything.

The Drug Nobody Talks About

Most people think addiction involves alcohol.

Drugs.

Pornography.

Gambling.

They're obvious addictions.

You can see them.

But there are more socially acceptable addictions that quietly destroy lives.

Approval.

Validation.

Being needed.

Being the hero.

Being the rescuer.

Being indispensable.

These addictions don't destroy your life quickly.

They destroy it slowly.

And because they often look noble from the outside, nobody notices.

Including you.

Especially you.

You convince yourself you're helping.

You convince yourself you're being selfless.

You convince yourself you're being a good husband.

A good father.

A good friend.

A good employee.

A good man.

Meanwhile, your entire identity becomes dependent upon what you can do for other people.

And that's where the trouble begins.

Because if your worth comes from what you do...

What happens when you stop doing?

What happens when somebody doesn't appreciate your sacrifices?

What happens when they leave?

What happens when your efforts aren't enough?

What happens when the people you've built your identity around no longer need you?

For many men, that's where the panic starts.

Not because they lost the relationship.

Because they lost the source of their value.

The Invisible Transaction

One of the most uncomfortable truths I had to confront was this:

Much of my giving wasn't actually unconditional.

That doesn't mean it wasn't genuine.

It doesn't mean I didn't love deeply.

It doesn't mean I was manipulating people.

It means there was often an invisible expectation attached to my generosity.

A hidden transaction.

The transaction sounded something like this:

"If I give enough, I'll feel valued."

"If I support enough, I'll feel appreciated."

"If I sacrifice enough, I'll feel loved."

The transaction wasn't conscious.

But it was there.

Most Nice Guys operate this way.

Not because they're bad people.

Because they don't believe they're enough without it.

The behaviour becomes a strategy.

A strategy designed to answer one question:

"How do I make sure I don't get rejected?"

The answer becomes:

Be useful.

Be needed.

Be indispensable.

Become so valuable that nobody would ever want to lose you.

Unfortunately, life doesn't work that way.

People leave.

People disappoint you.

People change.

Relationships evolve.

And when your identity is built around being needed, every one of those changes feels like a threat to your existence.

The Marriage Mirror

One of the greatest gifts of my life has been my marriage to Jana.

One of the hardest gifts too.

Because relationships have a brutal way of exposing the parts of ourselves we'd rather not see.

A good relationship doesn't create dysfunction.

It reveals it.

For years, I believed that loving harder was the answer to every relationship problem.

If there was tension?

Love harder.

If there was conflict?

Be more understanding.

If there was distance?

Give more.

If there was uncertainty?

Try harder.

That's what many men do.

We double down on effort.

We increase our sacrifice.

We become even more accommodating.

We become even more patient.

We become even more available.

And then we wonder why we feel exhausted.

Because effort cannot solve an identity problem.

The real issue wasn't that I didn't love enough.

The real issue was that I often measured my value through how much I could give.

That's a dangerous burden to place on a relationship.

Because eventually the relationship becomes responsible for validating your worth.

And no relationship can carry that weight forever.

No woman can.

No man can.

No marriage can.

That's too much responsibility to place on another human being.

The relationship wasn't supposed to tell me who I was.

I was supposed to know that before I entered it.

The Fatherhood Wake-Up Call

When Marinko was born, something changed inside me.

Every father knows this feeling.

One moment it's just you.

The next moment there's a little human being depending on you for everything.

And suddenly your heart exists outside your body.

Fatherhood amplifies everything.

Your strengths.

Your fears.

Your insecurities.

Your purpose.

And for a while, I did what many fathers do.

I threw myself into the role completely.

I wanted to be the best father possible.

The best husband possible.

The best provider possible.

Again, these are admirable goals.

The problem wasn't fatherhood.

The problem was that I was still measuring my value through performance.

The scorecard changed.

The pattern didn't.

I was still asking:

"Am I doing enough?"

"Am I giving enough?"

"Am I enough?"

Just in different ways.

Then one day my son asked me a question that stopped me cold.

"Daddy, do you think my brain is broken?"

That question hit me harder than almost anything else in my life.

Because I realised something.

I had spent most of my life asking the same question.

Not about my brain.

About myself.

Am I broken?

Am I enough?

Am I worthy?

Do I belong?

And in that moment I understood something profound.

The answer I gave my son had to become the answer I gave myself.

His worth wasn't conditional.

Neither was mine.

His value didn't need to be earned.

Neither did mine.

His existence made him worthy.

So did mine.

The Breakthrough

The biggest breakthrough of my life wasn't confidence.

It wasn't boundaries.

It wasn't masculinity.

It wasn't leadership.

It was worthiness.

It was finally understanding that my value wasn't something I needed to prove.

It was something I needed to recognise.

Think about how much of your life changes when you stop trying to earn your value.

You stop saying yes to things you hate.

You stop chasing approval.

You stop negotiating your standards.

You stop tolerating behaviour that violates your values.

You stop shrinking yourself to make others comfortable.

You stop treating your needs like an inconvenience.

Most importantly...

You stop living like a man desperately trying to justify his existence.

Because that's what many Nice Guys are really doing.

They're not seeking love.

They're seeking evidence that they're worthy of love.

There's a difference.

A massive difference.

One creates freedom.

The other creates dependency.

The Elevated Man

The Elevated Man still gives.

He still serves.

He still loves deeply.

He still protects.

He still contributes.

But his giving comes from abundance.

Not deficiency.

He doesn't help because he needs validation.

He helps because it aligns with his values.

He doesn't love because he's afraid of losing people.

He loves because that's who he is.

He doesn't lead because he wants control.

He leads because he accepts responsibility.

And perhaps most importantly...

He understands that his worth exists independently of the roles he plays.

Husband.

Father.

Provider.

Leader.

Friend.

These are expressions of who he is.

They are not who he is.

That's the distinction that changes everything.

The Elevated Man Challenge

Complete these sentences honestly:

I feel most valuable when __________.

I feel least valuable when __________.

I fear that without __________ I won't matter.

I secretly believe people love me because __________.

Now ask yourself:

Would I still be worthy if all of those things disappeared tomorrow?

Sit with that question.

Don't rush the answer.

Because hidden inside it may be the belief that has been running your life for decades.

And until you confront it, you'll continue trying to earn something that was already yours from the beginning.

CHAPTER THREE

The Approval Addiction

The invisible drug controlling your life

Most men don't realise they're addicted to approval.

I didn't.

If you'd asked me ten years ago whether I was an approval seeker, I would've laughed.

I wasn't posting shirtless selfies on Instagram.

I wasn't chasing popularity.

I wasn't trying to impress strangers.

I was a husband.

A father.

A provider.

A hard worker.

I wasn't looking for attention.

At least that's what I told myself.

The truth was much less obvious.

I wasn't addicted to attention.

I was addicted to acceptance.

And there's a big difference.

Attention says:

"Look at me."

Approval says:

"Please don't reject me."

One is loud.

The other is silent.

One is obvious.

The other quietly controls your life from the shadows.

And for most of my life, I had no idea it was there.

The World's Most Dangerous Drug

Imagine there was a drug that could instantly make you feel:

Accepted.

Valued.

Important.

Wanted.

Loved.

Respected.

How many people do you think would take it?

Most.

Maybe all.

The problem is that this drug already exists.

It's called approval.

And unlike alcohol, drugs, gambling, or pornography, society actively encourages it.

From the time we're children, we're trained to seek it.

Good boy.

Good student.

Good employee.

Good husband.

Good father.

Good citizen.

Good man.

We're rewarded when we conform.

Punished when we don't.

So we learn very quickly that acceptance feels good.

Rejection feels bad.

And before long, we begin organising our lives around avoiding rejection.

The trouble starts when avoiding rejection becomes more important than being ourselves.

That's when approval stops being normal and starts becoming an addiction.

The Prison Nobody Sees

The strange thing about approval addiction is that it doesn't feel like a prison.

It feels like responsibility.

It feels like maturity.

It feels like being considerate.

It feels like being a good person.

Which is exactly why it's so hard to recognise.

You don't notice it when you're constantly asking:

"What will people think?"

"Will this upset someone?"

"What if they don't agree?"

"What if they don't understand?"

"What if they get angry?"

"What if they leave?"

What you don't realise is that every one of those questions is pointing away from yourself.

Not one asks:

"What do I think?"

"What do I want?"

"What do I believe?"

"What aligns with my values?"

Approval addiction disconnects a man from his own internal compass.

He becomes so focused on everyone else's map that he forgets where he's trying to go.

And eventually he reaches a destination he never chose.

The Approval Economy

Here's something most men never realise.

Every day they're trading pieces of themselves for approval.

A little honesty here.

A little authenticity there.

A boundary.

An opinion.

A desire.

A dream.

A standard.

One compromise doesn't seem like much.

Neither does the second.

Or the third.

But years later those tiny compromises become a life.

A life built around managing other people's perceptions.

A life that looks successful from the outside but feels strangely empty on the inside.

Because deep down you know something isn't right.

You know you're performing.

You know you're filtering.

You know you're editing yourself.

And the worst part?

You often become so good at performing that even the people closest to you don't know who you really are.

Including you.

The Version Everybody Likes

One of the hardest truths I had to confront was that many people loved a version of me that wasn't entirely real.

Not because I was dishonest.

Because I was edited.

Filtered.

Softened.

Polished.

Conflict-free.

I had become skilled at presenting the version of myself most likely to maintain harmony.

The version least likely to upset people.

The version most likely to receive approval.

Many Nice Guys become masters of this.

They're social chameleons.

Put them in one room and they become one version of themselves.

Put them somewhere else and they become another.

They adapt.

Adjust.

Accommodate.

Blend in.

The irony is that the more approval they receive, the more disconnected they feel.

Because approval received for a performance never satisfies.

It can't.

Why?

Because deep down you know they aren't fully accepting you.

They're accepting the character you're playing.

And no amount of approval can fill that hole.

The Day I Stopped Asking Permission

One of the biggest changes in my life wasn't becoming more confident.

It was becoming more decisive.

Not because I suddenly knew all the answers.

I didn't.

Not because I stopped making mistakes.

I haven't.

The shift happened when I stopped asking permission to be myself.

For years I unconsciously looked outside myself before making decisions.

What will they think?

Will they approve?

Am I being selfish?

Is this okay?

The Alpha Code forced me to confront a different question.

What do I think?

That sounds simple.

It's not.

For a man who has spent decades outsourcing his self-worth, it's revolutionary.

Because the moment you start trusting your own judgement, your entire life changes.

You become harder to manipulate.

Harder to guilt.

Harder to control.

Harder to shame.

Not because you're arrogant.

Because you're grounded.

And grounded men don't need constant reassurance.

Why Approval Never Works

Let's assume you get everything you want.

Everybody likes you.

Nobody criticises you.

Nobody disagrees with you.

Nobody gets upset.

Nobody rejects you.

Sounds great, right?

Wrong.

Because now you've become a prisoner of maintaining that image.

Every interaction becomes a performance.

Every decision becomes political.

Every conversation becomes calculated.

You stop asking:

"What is true?"

And start asking:

"What is safest?"

That's not freedom.

That's emotional slavery.

And here's the kicker.

No matter how hard you try, somebody will eventually dislike you anyway.

You could dedicate your entire life to pleasing everyone and still end up criticised.

Ask any leader.

Any entrepreneur.

Any parent.

Any husband.

Any man trying to build something meaningful.

Disapproval is not a possibility.

It's a certainty.

Which means approval can never be a reliable foundation for your life.

Because you're building your identity on something you can't control.

The Courage To Disappoint

One of the most liberating lessons I ever learned was this:

Disappointing people isn't always a sign you're doing something wrong.

Sometimes it's evidence you're finally being honest.

That idea was deeply uncomfortable for me.

Because I'd spent years believing that keeping people happy was my responsibility.

It's not.

Your responsibility is to act with integrity.

To tell the truth.

To honour your values.

To communicate clearly.

To lead yourself.

How other people respond is their responsibility.

Not yours.

That doesn't mean you become selfish.

It doesn't mean you stop caring.

It means you stop carrying emotional responsibilities that never belonged to you in the first place.

And that distinction changes everything.

The Approval Detox

The moment you stop seeking approval, something strange happens.

At first, anxiety increases.

People notice the changes.

They notice the new boundaries.

The new honesty.

The new standards.

Some people won't like it.

Good.

That means it's working.

Because growth often feels like rejection to people who benefited from the old version of you.

Read that again.

Growth often feels like rejection to people who benefited from the old version of you.

Not everyone will celebrate your evolution.

Some people preferred the version of you that always said yes.

The version that never challenged them.

The version that abandoned himself for their convenience.

That's okay.

You're not building your life around approval anymore.

You're building it around truth.

The Elevated Man

The Elevated Man understands something most men never do.

Approval is not confidence.

Approval is not self-worth.

Approval is not love.

Approval is not respect.

Approval is simply somebody else's opinion.

Nothing more. Nothing less.

He understands that his value cannot rise or fall based on external validation.

He doesn't need permission to pursue his mission.

He doesn't need consensus to honour his standards.

He doesn't need universal agreement to speak the truth.

He respects others.

But he doesn't outsource his identity to them.

Most importantly, he understands that self-respect and approval often move in opposite directions.

The moment you start telling the truth, someone will be disappointed.

The moment you start setting boundaries, someone will be frustrated.

The moment you start prioritising your values, someone will disagree.

That's not failure.

That's adulthood.

The Elevated Man Challenge

For the next seven days, pay attention to every decision you make.

Ask yourself:

"Am I doing this because it aligns with my values?"

Or:

"Am I doing this to gain approval or avoid disapproval?"

Be brutally honest.

No judgement.

No shame.

Just awareness.

At the end of the week, review your answers.

You may discover that much of your life has been built around avoiding rejection rather than pursuing truth.

And if that's the case, don't beat yourself up.

Most men never notice it.

You're already ahead of them.

Because freedom begins the moment you realise you've been living inside a prison.

And approval is one of the most comfortable prisons ever built.

CHAPTER FOUR

Losing Yourself While Loving Others

When love turns into self-abandonment

The greatest irony of my life is that the thing I valued most was also the thing I nearly lost.

My marriage.

Not because I didn't love my wife.

Not because I wasn't committed.

Not because I wasn't trying.

The truth is far more uncomfortable.

I nearly lost my marriage because I was trying too hard.

Now, before you roll your eyes and think that's the dumbest thing you've read all year, hear me out.

Because this is a mistake millions of men make.

Especially good men.

Especially caring men.

Especially family men.

The men who love deeply.

The men who would walk through fire for the people they care about.

The men who genuinely want to do the right thing.

Men like me.

The problem isn't that we don't love enough.

The problem is that we sometimes love in a way that slowly erodes our sense of self.

And when that happens, the relationship suffers anyway.

Not immediately.

Slowly.

Quietly.

Almost invisibly.

Like rust.

The Day I Met Jana

I still remember the first time I saw Jana.

It was 28 March 2005.

Mandurah Foreshore.

I saw this stunning woman walking with her friends.

And when I say stunning, I mean the kind of beautiful that makes your brain temporarily stop functioning.

I panicked.

Completely panicked.

My smooth and sophisticated strategy was to throw my phone number out the car window and drive away.

Looking back, it's amazing that strategy worked at all.

Fortunately, Jana's friend Laura picked up the number and called me.

That phone call changed my life.

For twenty years Jana has been my greatest adventure.

We've travelled together.

Built a life together.

Built a home together.

Got married in Croatia.

Raised our beautiful son.

Created a life that younger me could only dream about.

She's been my greatest supporter.

My closest friend.

My safe place.

And that's exactly why this chapter matters.

Because loving someone deeply does not make you immune from losing yourself.

In fact, it often increases the risk.

When Love Becomes Identity

When people hear the phrase "losing yourself in a relationship," they usually imagine something dramatic.

A controlling partner.

Isolation.

Manipulation.

Toxicity.

Sometimes that's true.

But often it happens in a much quieter way.

You simply start placing the relationship at the centre of your identity.

The relationship becomes the sun.

Everything else begins orbiting around it.

Your goals.

Your hobbies.

Your friendships.

Your ambitions.

Your standards.

Your needs.

Your opinions.

Slowly, they all start moving further away from the centre.

And because it happens gradually, you barely notice.

You tell yourself you're being devoted.

Committed.

Loving.

Supportive.

And maybe you are.

But devotion without self-respect eventually becomes self-abandonment.

That's what I couldn't see.

I thought being a good husband meant sacrificing more.

Giving more.

Trying harder.

Being more understanding.

Being more accommodating.

Being more available.

I believed that if I loved hard enough, everything would work itself out.

Unfortunately, relationships don't reward self-abandonment.

They expose it.

The Slow Disappearance

Nobody wakes up one morning and says:

"Today I'm going to abandon myself."

It happens one decision at a time.

You don't speak up about something that bothers you.

You let it go.

You tell yourself it's not important.

Then you do it again.

And again.

And again.

You start filtering your opinions.

Avoiding difficult conversations.

Suppressing frustrations.

Trying to keep the peace.

Trying to avoid conflict.

Trying to maintain harmony.

At first it seems harmless.

Mature even.

But every time you silence yourself, a small piece of self-trust disappears.

Every time you betray your own truth, your confidence weakens.

Not because someone else did something wrong.

Because your subconscious notices.

It sees every compromise.

Every silence.

Every betrayal.

And eventually it stops trusting you.

Many men think confidence comes from success.

It doesn't.

Confidence comes from self-trust.

And self-trust is impossible when you keep abandoning yourself.

The Hidden Contract

Most Nice Guys carry an invisible contract.

I certainly did.

The contract sounds something like this:

"If I love enough, she'll love me."

"If I sacrifice enough, she'll appreciate me."

"If I support enough, she'll understand me."

"If I'm patient enough, everything will eventually improve."

The problem is that relationships don't operate on hidden contracts.

Nobody knows the deal you've made inside your own head.

And when reality fails to meet those expectations, resentment appears.

Resentment is one of the most misunderstood emotions in relationships.

People think resentment means anger.

It doesn't.

Resentment is grief.

It's the pain of abandoning yourself over and over again and not receiving the outcome you hoped for.

It's emotional debt.

And eventually the bill arrives.

The Near Divorce

There was a period when my marriage was hanging by a thread.

From the outside people probably wouldn't have known.

Most struggling couples become experts at looking okay.

But beneath the surface, things were breaking down.

Not because love had disappeared.

The love was still there.

The problem was that somewhere along the way I had lost myself.

And when a man loses himself, everyone around him feels it.

His confidence changes.

His energy changes.

His leadership changes.

His presence changes.

His emotional stability changes.

Everything changes.

The relationship begins carrying responsibilities it was never designed to carry.

I was asking the relationship to provide certainty.

Identity.

Validation.

Worth.

Security.

No relationship can sustain that burden forever.

The marriage wasn't failing because there wasn't enough love.

The marriage was struggling because I wasn't bringing a complete version of myself into it.

I was bringing a man who had forgotten who he was.

The Mirror

Relationships are mirrors.

Painful mirrors.

Beautiful mirrors.

Unforgiving mirrors.

They show us exactly where we're strong.

And exactly where we're underdeveloped.

For years I thought relationship problems were something to solve externally.

Communication.

Behaviour.

Conflict.

Compromise.

What I eventually realised was that many of my relationship problems were actually identity problems.

I wasn't struggling because Jana was wrong.

I was struggling because I had disconnected from myself.

That's a difficult truth.

Because it removes the ability to blame.

And when blame disappears, responsibility appears.

Responsibility isn't always comfortable.

But it's incredibly empowering.

Because if you're responsible, you can change it.

The Alpha Code Breakthrough

The 90 day Alpha Code course created by Justin Dulihanty, the founder of the Men's Development Academy, didn't save my marriage.

I did.

Jana did.

We did.

The Alpha Code simply gave me the tools to see what was actually happening.

For the first time, I started asking different questions.

Not:

"How do I make this relationship better?"

But:

"Who am I becoming inside this relationship?"

Not:

"What does Jana need from me?"

But:

"What do I need from myself?"

Not:

"How do I keep everyone happy?"

But:

"What aligns with my values?"

Those questions changed everything.

Because they forced me to reconnect with the man underneath the husband.

The man underneath the father.

The man underneath the provider.

The man underneath the people-pleaser.

For the first time in years, I started coming home to myself.

The Return of Cade

One of the most profound realisations I had was this:

The man Jana originally fell in love with wasn't trying to please everyone.

He wasn't seeking permission.

He wasn't constantly second-guessing himself.

He was confident enough to throw his number out a car window and risk rejection.

That version of me still existed.

He was just buried under years of responsibility, pressure, expectations, fear, and self-abandonment.

The goal wasn't to become someone new.

The goal was to recover who I'd always been.

I think many men misunderstand personal development.

They think it's about adding.

More confidence.

More discipline.

More skills.

More success.

Most of the time it's about removing.

Removing fear.

Removing shame.

Removing conditioning.

Removing masks.

Removing everything that isn't really you.

And underneath all of it, you find the man you've been searching for.

Love Without Losing Yourself

Today my marriage is stronger than it's ever been.

Not because we're perfect.

Not because we never disagree.

Not because life became easier.

It's stronger because I stopped trying to earn love and started bringing my authentic self into the relationship.

I became more honest.

More grounded.

More decisive.

More authentic.

More connected to my values.

Ironically, becoming more myself improved the relationship.

Because healthy relationships don't require self-abandonment.

They require self-awareness.

The strongest marriages are not built by two people losing themselves in each other.

They're built by two whole people choosing each other every day.

That's a very different thing.

One is dependency.

The other is love.

The Elevated Man

The Elevated Man understands something many men never learn.

Love is not measured by how much of yourself you're willing to sacrifice.

Love is measured by how fully you can show up.

Present.

Authentic.

Grounded.

Honest.

Whole.

He doesn't disappear inside the people he loves.

He doesn't make his partner responsible for his self-worth.

He doesn't abandon himself to maintain harmony.

He loves deeply.

But he remains connected to himself while doing it.

That's the difference between attachment and love.

Attachment says:

"I need you to complete me."

Love says:

"I choose you while remaining complete myself."

One creates dependency.

The other creates freedom.

The Elevated Man Challenge

Answer the following questions honestly:

What parts of yourself have you sacrificed in order to maintain a relationship?

What opinions do you routinely suppress?

What needs do you feel guilty expressing?

What conversations have you been avoiding?

Who were you before you started editing yourself to keep others comfortable?

Now ask yourself the most important question of all:

Are you loving from strength?

Or are you loving from fear?

Because those two things may look identical on the surface.

But they create completely different lives.

And completely different relationships.

PART II
REBUILDING THE FOUNDATION
Creating The Man Beneath The Masks

CHAPTER FIVE

The Inner Architect

Designing a life instead of drifting through one

Most men spend their lives living by default.

Not because they're lazy.

Not because they're weak.

Not because they lack ambition.

They live by default because nobody ever taught them how to live by design.

Think about it.

You spend years learning mathematics.

Science.

History.

Geography.

How to drive a car.

How to use a computer.

How to earn money.

Yet nobody sits you down and teaches you arguably the most important skill you'll ever need:

How to consciously build a life.

So most people don't.

They drift.

They react.

They adapt.

They survive.

Then one day they wake up at forty, fifty, or sixty years old and realise they've spent decades building a life they never intentionally chose.

They followed expectations.

Social norms.

Family conditioning.

Fear.

Approval.

Obligation.

And somewhere along the way they forgot to ask a very important question:

What do I actually want?

That question changed my life.

The House I Never Designed

Imagine hiring a builder to construct your dream home.

On the first day he arrives and asks:

"Where are the plans?"

You shrug.

"I don't have any."

"Okay," he says. "What does the house look like?"

"No idea."

"How many bedrooms?"

"Haven't thought about it."

"What style?"

"Whatever."

"What outcome are we building toward?"

"I'll know it when I see it."

You'd think he was dealing with a lunatic.

Yet this is exactly how many people approach their lives.

No vision.

No direction.

No blueprint.

No destination.

Then they wonder why they feel lost.

You cannot build a meaningful life without a vision any more than you can build a house without plans.

And that was one of the biggest lessons I learned through my own transformation.

If you don't consciously choose your direction, life will choose it for you.

Usually based on other people's expectations.

Why Most Men Feel Lost

When men tell me they feel lost, stuck, disconnected, or uncertain, I rarely believe that's the real problem.

Lost isn't the problem.

Lost is the symptom.

The problem is usually lack of vision.

Because uncertainty creates anxiety.

Direction creates confidence.

Notice I didn't say success creates confidence.

Direction creates confidence.

A man moving toward a meaningful future often feels more confident than a man who has already achieved external success but doesn't know why he's doing it.

One man is growing.

The other is drifting.

Growth creates energy.

Drifting creates despair.

That's why so many men experience a crisis when they achieve everything they thought they wanted.

The house.

The marriage.

The career.

The income.

The possessions.

Then one day they sit quietly and think:

"Is this it?"

The problem wasn't achievement.

The problem was they never consciously designed the life they were pursuing.

The GPS In Your Head

One of the most fascinating concepts I learned was something called the Reticular Activating System, or RAS.

Think of it as the brain's filtering system.

Every second your senses are bombarded with millions of pieces of information.

Sounds.

Colours.

Conversations.

Sensations.

Thoughts.

If your brain consciously processed all of it, you'd lose your mind.

So the RAS acts like a filter.

It decides what's important and what's not.

Here's where things get interesting.

The RAS doesn't filter based on reality.

It filters based on focus.

Whatever you consistently focus on becomes easier to see.

If you believe you're unlucky, you'll find evidence.

If you believe you're not good enough, you'll find evidence.

If you believe relationships always fail, you'll find evidence.

Your brain becomes a detective searching for proof that your beliefs are true.

Most people unknowingly program their minds for failure.

They focus on what they fear.

What they don't want.

What could go wrong.

And then wonder why life feels negative.

The brain simply follows instructions.

The problem is that most people never consciously provide any.

The Future Self Exercise

One exercise completely changed how I viewed my life.

Instead of focusing on who I was, I started focusing on who I wanted to become.

Not what I wanted to own.

Who I wanted to be.

That's an important distinction.

Most goals fail because they're built around outcomes.

Money.

Cars.

Houses.

Achievements.

The problem is that outcomes don't create identity.

Identity creates outcomes.

The question isn't:

"What do I want to have?"

The question is:

"Who do I need to become?"

The day I started asking that question, everything shifted.

Because suddenly my focus moved away from my problems and toward my possibilities.

I wasn't trying to fix a broken man.

I was building a future one.

Meeting The Elevated Man

One of the most powerful exercises I ever completed was creating a detailed vision of my future self.

I imagined him clearly.

How he thought.

How he spoke.

How he treated people.

How he treated himself.

How he showed up as a husband.

As a father.

As a leader.

As a man.

The more specific I became, the more powerful the exercise became.

I began asking:

What standards does he live by?

What excuses has he eliminated?

How does he handle adversity?

What does he tolerate?

What does he refuse to tolerate?

How does he respond under pressure?

What would make him proud?

What would disappoint him?

Slowly, the image became clearer.

And something interesting happened.

The gap between who I was and who I wanted to become started guiding my decisions.

Not through shame.

Through direction.

Direction is incredibly powerful.

Because once you know where you're going, decision-making becomes easier.

Every choice either moves you toward the man you want to become.

Or away from him.

Why Vision Creates Confidence

Most people think confidence comes from achievement.

I don't.

I think confidence comes from evidence.

Evidence that you're becoming the person you said you would become.

Confidence grows every time you keep your word to yourself.

Every workout.

Every boundary.

Every difficult conversation.

Every promise kept.

Every courageous decision.

Every aligned action.

That's why confidence cannot be purchased.

It cannot be downloaded.

It cannot be faked.

It must be earned through action.

Not action designed to impress others.

Action aligned with your vision.

That's real confidence.

And real confidence is surprisingly quiet.

It doesn't need validation.

Because it already knows where it's going.

Stop Fixing Yourself

One of the biggest mistakes people make in personal development is viewing themselves as projects that need fixing.

I understand why.

I did it too.

We focus on weaknesses.

Flaws.

Deficits.

Trauma.

Mistakes.

Problems.

The entire process becomes one giant self-improvement mission.

The danger is that if you're always fixing yourself, you unconsciously reinforce the belief that you're broken.

You're not.

You may be wounded.

Conditioned.

Misguided.

Fearful.

Confused.

But broken?

No.

You're a human being.

And human beings don't need fixing.

They need direction.

Most men don't need to become someone else.

They need to become more of who they already are.

That's a completely different journey.

The Elevated Man Blueprint

When I think about The Elevated Man today, I don't think about status.

I don't think about money.

I don't think about dominance.

I think about alignment.

The Elevated Man knows who he is.

He knows what he values.

He knows where he's going.

His life reflects his standards.

His actions support his vision.

His choices align with his code.

He's not perfect.

He still fails.

He still struggles.

He still doubts himself.

But he no longer drifts.

Because direction is more important than perfection.

Always.

The Elevated Man Challenge

Find a quiet place.

Turn off your phone.

Grab a notebook.

Answer these questions:

Who do I want to become in ten years?

What kind of husband do I want to be?

What kind of father do I want to be?

What kind of leader do I want to be?

What kind of man do I want people to describe when I'm gone?

What standards does that man live by?

What habits does he practice daily?

What behaviours has he eliminated?

Now write one sentence.

A sentence that describes the future version of yourself.

Not who you are.

Who you're becoming.

Make it powerful.

Make it honest.

Make it yours.

Because the moment you create a vision, something remarkable happens.

Your life stops being something that happens to you.

And starts becoming something you intentionally build.

That is where transformation begins.

Not with motivation.

Not with confidence.

Not with success.

With vision.

Every great structure begins with a blueprint.

And every great man begins with a decision.

A decision to stop drifting and start designing.

CHAPTER SIX

Who The Hell Are You

The search for identity beneath the roles

Most men can tell you what they do.

Few can tell you who they are.

Think about it.

Meet someone new and within thirty seconds the conversation usually sounds something like this:

"What do you do?"

"I'm an electrician."

"I'm a manager."

"I'm a business owner."

"I'm a teacher."

"I'm a tradesman."

"I'm a father."

"I'm a husband."

Those aren't identities.

Those are roles.

And roles are dangerous things to build your life around.

Because roles change.

Jobs change.

Businesses fail.

Children grow up.

Relationships end.

Careers evolve.

Life happens.

And if your identity is built on roles, every major life change feels like an identity crisis.

Because it is.

The question underneath every personal development journey is not:

"How do I become successful?"

It's not:

"How do I become confident?"

It's not even:

"How do I become a better man?"

The real question is:

Who the hell am I?

It's a simple question.

It's also one of the hardest questions you'll ever answer.

The Masks We Wear

Most men don't realise how many masks they wear.

I certainly didn't.

For years, I thought I was simply being adaptable.

Professional at work.

Supportive at home.

Reliable with friends.

Responsible as a father.

Strong during difficult times.

But eventually I realised something uncomfortable.

Some of those weren't adaptations.

They were disguises.

Masks designed to gain approval.

Masks designed to avoid rejection.

Masks designed to keep the peace.

Masks designed to make sure everybody liked me.

The problem with wearing masks is that eventually you forget where the mask ends and you begin.

You become so good at performing that you lose access to your authentic self.

And here's the really dangerous part.

The mask usually works.

People like it.

People praise it.

People reward it.

Which makes it even harder to remove.

Because the moment you start being authentic, some people won't like the real version of you.

That's terrifying.

Until you realise something important.

The people who only like the mask never really knew you anyway.

The Identity Theft Nobody Talks About

When most people hear the phrase identity theft, they think of criminals stealing credit cards.

That's not the identity theft I'm talking about.

The identity theft I'm talking about happens much earlier.

It's when you slowly surrender pieces of yourself to fit into other people's expectations.

A little piece here.

A little piece there.

You stop expressing an opinion.

You suppress a desire.

You abandon a dream.

You ignore a value.

You tolerate behaviour that violates your standards.

Not because you want to.

Because you want acceptance.

Eventually the theft becomes so gradual that you don't even notice it's happening.

Until one day you wake up feeling disconnected from your own life.

Many men describe this feeling as being lost.

I don't think they're lost.

I think they're disconnected from themselves.

There's a difference.

Lost means you don't know where you are.

Disconnected means you've forgotten who you are.

The Day I Asked The Wrong Question

For most of my life, I asked questions like:

What do people expect from me?

What should I do?

What would a good husband do?

What would a good father do?

What would a good man do?

At first glance, those seem like noble questions.

The problem is they all focus outward.

They focus on expectations.

Responsibilities.

Perceptions.

Roles.

Not identity.

Not values.

Not truth.

Eventually I realised I had been asking the wrong question.

The question wasn't:

"What should I do?"

The question was:

"Who do I want to be?"

Everything changed when I understood that.

Because behaviour becomes much easier when identity is clear.

If you know who you are, decisions become simpler.

If you know what you stand for, boundaries become easier.

If you know your values, leadership becomes natural.

Confusion disappears when identity appears.

Values: The Invisible Operating System

Most people have never intentionally chosen their values.

They've inherited them.

From parents.

Schools.

Culture.

Religion.

Friends.

Social media.

Society.

The problem isn't that inherited values are bad.

The problem is that many people never examine them.

They simply assume they're theirs.

Imagine buying a computer and discovering somebody else had programmed the operating system.

You'd probably want to check what software was running.

Yet most people never do this with their own beliefs.

They spend decades operating under rules they never consciously chose.

Rules like:

Don't upset people.

Always be nice.

Avoid conflict.

Don't be selfish.

Put others first.

Stay safe.

Fit in.

Be realistic.

Some of these beliefs may serve you.

Others may be quietly sabotaging your life.

The Elevated Man questions everything.

Not because he's rebellious.

Because he's conscious.

He understands that an examined life is a powerful life.

An unexamined life is simply conditioning.

Your Personal Code

One of the biggest breakthroughs in my journey came when I stopped focusing on goals and started focusing on standards.

Goals are temporary.

Standards are permanent.

A goal says:

"I want to lose ten kilos."

A standard says:

"I take care of my body."

A goal says:

"I want a better marriage."

A standard says:

"I communicate honestly and lead with integrity."

A goal says:

"I want confidence."

A standard says:

"I keep my word to myself."

Do you see the difference?

Goals can be achieved and forgotten.

Standards become part of who you are.

The Elevated Man doesn't build his life around goals.

He builds it around a code.

A personal code.

A set of principles that guide his behaviour regardless of circumstances.

Because circumstances change.

Values shouldn't.

The Elevated Man Code

Every man's code will be different.

But mine eventually came down to a handful of principles.

Tell the truth.

Take responsibility.

Keep your word.

Choose courage over comfort.

Love without losing yourself.

Set boundaries without guilt.

Feel everything be ruled by nothing.

Become the man you needed.

Lead yourself first.

Leave people better than you found them.

Protect what matters.

Never stop becoming.

Simple.

Not easy.

But simple.

The power of a code is that it removes confusion.

When life gets difficult, you don't ask:

"What do I feel like doing?"

You ask:

"What does my code require?"

Feelings fluctuate.

Values endure.

That's what makes them so powerful.

The Man In The Mirror

A lot of men spend years trying to become somebody.

I did too.

Stronger.

More successful.

More confident.

More respected.

More masculine.

There's nothing wrong with growth.

Growth is important.

But eventually I realised I was chasing something I already possessed.

Worth.

The man I was trying to become wasn't waiting for me in the future.

He was buried underneath fear.

Underneath conditioning.

Underneath approval-seeking.

Underneath self-doubt.

Underneath people-pleasing.

The journey wasn't about creating a new identity.

It was about uncovering the authentic one.

That's why self-discovery matters.

You can't become yourself if you don't know who that is.

And most men don't.

Not because they're incapable.

Because nobody ever taught them how.

Identity Before Behaviour

This is where many personal development programs get it wrong.

They focus on behaviour first.

Wake up earlier.

Work harder.

Be more disciplined.

Take more action.

None of those things are bad.

But behaviour rarely changes permanently without identity.

If a smoker is trying to quit smoking, what creates lasting change?

Saying:

"I'm trying not to smoke."

Or saying:

"I'm not a smoker."

One focuses on behaviour.

The other focuses on identity.

Identity drives behaviour.

Always.

The moment you decide who you are, your behaviour starts aligning with that decision.

That's why this chapter matters.

Because before you build confidence, leadership, discipline, or success.

You need to know who the hell you're building them for.

The Elevated Man

The Elevated Man knows who he is.

Not perfectly.

Not completely.

But clearly.

He knows his values.

His standards.

His mission.

His principles.

His code.

He doesn't borrow identity from his career.

His relationship.

His income.

His achievements.

Those things may enhance his life.

But they do not define it.

He understands that character is what remains when everything else is stripped away.

And character is where true confidence lives.

Not in success.

Not in status.

Not in approval.

In identity.

The Elevated Man Challenge

Take a blank page and write answers to the following questions.

What do I stand for?

What do I refuse to tolerate?

What qualities do I admire most in men?

What behaviours make me proud of myself?

What behaviours disappoint me?

What principles would I want my son to live by?

What principles would I want people to describe at my funeral?

Now create your Personal Code.

Five to ten statements.

Simple.

Clear.

Non-negotiable.

Not goals.

Standards.

Not outcomes.

Identity.

Because every great man lives by a code.

The question is whether you've consciously chosen yours.

Or whether you're still living by somebody else's.

And until you answer that question, you'll continue searching for yourself in places you'll never find him.

The man you're looking for isn't out there.

He's already inside you.

It's time to meet him.

CHAPTER SEVEN

The Death Of Performance

Ending the exhausting need to prove yourself

For most of my life, I lived like I was standing on a stage.

I didn't know it at the time.

In fact, if someone had accused me of performing, I probably would've argued with them.

I wasn't an actor.

I wasn't fake.

I wasn't pretending to be someone I wasn't.

At least I didn't think I was.

The truth was more subtle than that.

I wasn't performing for attention.

I was performing for worth.

And there's a huge difference.

One says:

"Look at me."

The other says:

"Please tell me I'm enough."

That was the game I had been playing for years.

Maybe decades.

Not consciously.

Very few men do it consciously.

But looking back, I can see it everywhere.

I performed through achievement.

Through sacrifice.

Through responsibility.

Through loyalty.

Through being dependable.

Through being needed.

Through being useful.

Through being the good man.

And the strange thing is, the world rewards that behaviour.

People admire it.

Respect it.

Celebrate it.

Which makes it incredibly difficult to see the trap.

Because the trap doesn't look like failure.

It often looks like success.

The Invisible Audition

Imagine waking up every morning and believing you have to audition for your place in the world.

Not once.

Every day.

You have to prove you're a good husband.

Prove you're a good father.

Prove you're a good employee.

Prove you're a good leader.

Prove you're a good man.

Prove you're worthy.

Prove you belong.

Prove you matter.

Sounds exhausting, doesn't it?

That's because it is.

Yet millions of men are doing exactly that.

Every single day.

They're not living.

They're auditioning.

Every interaction becomes a test.

Every setback becomes evidence they're failing.

Every criticism becomes confirmation they're not enough.

And because the standard is impossible, the performance never ends.

You can never finally relax.

Never finally arrive.

Never finally be enough.

Because the goalpost keeps moving.

That's what performance-based worth does.

It creates a game you cannot win.

The Day I Realised Success Wasn't Working

One of the most confusing experiences a man can have is achieving something he desperately wanted and still feeling empty afterward.

We've all experienced it.

The promotion.

The house.

The relationship.

The achievement.

The milestone.

You spend months or years pursuing it.

Convinced it will finally make you feel different.

Then you achieve it.

And for a brief moment, it does.

You feel excited.

Proud.

Validated.

Accomplished.

Then something strange happens.

The feeling fades.

And you're right back where you started.

Looking for the next thing.

The next achievement.

The next validation hit.

The next reason to feel worthy.

I spent years trapped in that cycle.

Not because I was greedy.

Because I was searching for something achievement could never provide.

Self-worth.

The problem with external validation is that it only works externally.

It never reaches the wound underneath.

The Bucket With A Hole In It

Imagine trying to fill a bucket with water.

Except the bucket has a hole in the bottom.

You pour more water in.

The bucket empties.

So you pour more.

Still empty.

More.

Still empty.

That's what life feels like when your self-worth depends on performance.

No achievement is ever enough.

No amount of praise is enough.

No amount of success is enough.

No amount of validation is enough.

Because you're trying to solve an internal problem with external solutions.

And external solutions can never fill an internal void.

I know.

I tried.

For years.

The Question Beneath Every Question

After my suicide attempt, I spent a lot of time reflecting on my life.

Not because I suddenly became enlightened.

Because surviving has a way of forcing you to ask uncomfortable questions.

Questions you can normally avoid.

Questions that cut straight through the bullshit.

Questions like:

Who am I?

Why am I here?

What actually matters?

What am I chasing?

What am I trying to prove?

Eventually I discovered something.

Almost every struggle in my life traced back to one question.

Am I enough?

That question was hiding underneath everything.

The people-pleasing.

The perfectionism.

The over-giving.

The conflict avoidance.

The need to be needed.

The desire for approval.

The fear of rejection.

All of it.

Different symptoms.

Same wound.

Am I enough?

It's a question many men never consciously ask.

Yet they spend their entire lives trying to answer it.

The Great Lie

There is one lie more destructive than almost any other.

The lie says:

"You become worthy when..."

When you succeed.

When you achieve.

When you earn enough.

When you get married.

When you become a father.

When you get fit.

When you gain confidence.

When people respect you.

When people admire you.

When people choose you.

When people approve of you.

The details vary.

The lie remains the same.

Worthiness becomes conditional.

Always dependent upon some future outcome.

Some future achievement.

Some future version of yourself.

And because that version never fully arrives, worthiness remains forever out of reach.

It's psychological torture disguised as self-improvement.

The tragedy is that most men don't realise they're living inside it.

The Lesson My Son Taught Me

One day my son asked me a question.

"Daddy, do you think my brain is broken?"

That question hit me harder than he could ever understand.

Because in that moment I realised something.

If Marinko had asked:

"Daddy, am I enough?"

My answer would've been immediate.

Of course you are.

I wouldn't ask about his grades.

His achievements.

His behaviour.

His future success.

His performance.

None of it.

His worth would be unquestionable.

Immediate.

Absolute.

Because he's my son.

And because he's human.

Then a disturbing thought appeared.

Why was I willing to give him the compassion I refused to give myself?

Why did he deserve unconditional worthiness but I didn't?

That question haunted me.

And eventually it transformed me.

Because I realised something incredibly simple.

If worthiness is inherent in him, it's inherent in me too.

And it's inherent in you.

The Death Of The Old Identity

Every transformation requires a death.

Not a physical death.

An identity death.

The old version of you must die so the new version can emerge.

For me, the identity that had to die was the performer.

The man who believed he had to earn love.

Earn respect.

Earn belonging.

Earn approval.

Earn worth.

That man was exhausted.

He spent decades proving himself.

And no amount of proving ever felt like enough.

Eventually I stopped asking:

"What do I need to do to be worthy?"

And started asking:

"What if I already am?"

That single question changed my life.

Because if I was already worthy...

I could stop performing.

I could stop proving.

I could stop negotiating my value.

I could stop living like I was on trial.

For the first time in my life, I could simply be.

What Happens When You Stop Performing

Something remarkable happens when a man no longer needs validation.

He becomes honest.

Not brutally honest.

Not arrogant.

Not selfish.

Simply honest.

He says what he thinks.

He asks for what he needs.

He sets boundaries.

He tells the truth.

He makes decisions.

He accepts disagreement.

He survives disapproval.

He trusts himself.

Not because he's fearless.

Because his worth is no longer on the line.

The moment worthiness becomes internal, freedom appears.

And freedom changes everything.

The Elevated Man

The Elevated Man understands a truth that most men spend their lives avoiding.

His value is not determined by:

His income.

His title.

His status.

His possessions.

His achievements.

His relationship.

His popularity.

His productivity.

His usefulness.

His value comes from his humanity.

His character.

His integrity.

His existence.

Everything else is simply an expression of that worth.

Not proof of it.

That's the distinction.

And it's one of the most liberating distinctions a man can ever make.

Because the moment he stops trying to earn his worth, he becomes free to express it.

The Elevated Man Challenge

Take a blank page.

Write down every sentence that begins with:

"I'll be enough when..."

Don't overthink it.

Just write.

I'll be enough when I lose weight.

I'll be enough when I make more money.

I'll be enough when my marriage improves.

I'll be enough when people respect me.

I'll be enough when I'm more confident.

Write them all down.

Then look at the list.

Read every sentence.

One by one.

And replace it with:

"I am already enough. Growth is simply how I express it."

Read them out loud.

You may not believe it yet.

That's okay.

Most men don't.

Not at first.

Because you've spent years being taught otherwise.

But eventually the truth begins to sink in.

You don't need to become worthy.

You already are.

And from that moment forward, everything changes.

Not because you stopped growing.

Because you finally stopped trying to earn the right to exist.

And that's where the real journey begins.

PART III

THE WAR WITHIN

Confronting The Inner Battles

CHAPTER EIGHT

The Emotional Prison

The feelings you've spent years avoiding

Most men aren't trapped by their emotions.

They're trapped by their fear of emotions.

That's an important distinction.

Because for most of my life, I thought my emotions were the enemy.

Sadness was weakness.

Anxiety was something to push through.

Fear was something to suppress.

Pain was something to ignore.

If something hurt, I buried it.

If something bothered me, I minimised it.

If something scared me, I pretended it didn't.

Like many men, I became incredibly skilled at emotional avoidance.

And here's the funny thing.

Society often rewards that behaviour.

The guy who keeps moving.

The guy who never complains.

The guy who stays strong.

The guy who handles everything.

The guy who puts his head down and gets on with it.

We call him resilient.

Sometimes he is.

Sometimes he's simply disconnected.

There's a difference.

A huge difference.

Because resilience is feeling pain and continuing forward.

Avoidance is pretending the pain isn't there.

And what you refuse to feel doesn't disappear.

It waits.

The Basement

Imagine your mind is a house.

Every painful emotion you don't want to deal with gets thrown into the basement.

Fear?

Basement.

Shame?

Basement.

Grief?

Basement.

Anger?

Basement.

Loneliness?

Basement.

Rejection?

Basement.

Humiliation?

Basement.

You keep throwing things down there because you don't want them upstairs where you can see them.

The problem is that emotions don't die in the basement.

They multiply.

And eventually the basement becomes so full that it starts affecting the entire house.

You become irritable.

Anxious.

Withdrawn.

Reactive.

Numb.

Depressed.

Exhausted.

Not because you're weak.

Because you're carrying emotional weight you never processed.

Many men spend decades dragging around emotional baggage they refuse to unpack.

Then wonder why life feels heavy.

The Weight I Couldn't Carry

There was a period of my life when everything felt heavy.

Not physically.

Emotionally.

Every day felt harder than it should.

Everything required effort.

Simple tasks felt overwhelming.

Joy felt distant.

Hope felt faint.

The strange thing about depression is that it rarely announces itself.

It doesn't kick the front door down.

It quietly moves into your house and rearranges the furniture.

One day you realise you don't recognise your own life anymore.

You stop looking forward to things.

You stop feeling connected.

You stop feeling like yourself.

And perhaps most dangerously, you stop believing things can change.

Depression isn't always overwhelming sadness.

Sometimes it's the absence of feeling.

The absence of hope.

The absence of energy.

The absence of possibility.

Eventually I found myself in a place darker than I ever imagined possible.

Looking back now, I can see something I couldn't see then.

The depression wasn't just about circumstances.

It wasn't just about stress.

It wasn't just about life.

It was years of emotional suppression finally demanding attention.

Years of carrying things I never allowed myself to feel.

Men Don't Talk About This

One of the greatest tragedies of modern masculinity is that many men have been taught to fear their emotional world.

Not intentionally.

Most people mean well.

But somewhere along the way many of us absorbed messages like:

Be strong.

Don't cry.

Man up.

Get over it.

Move on.

Toughen up.

Again, resilience matters.

Mental toughness matters.

Personal responsibility matters.

But emotional suppression is not strength.

It's avoidance disguised as strength.

The strongest men I know are not emotionally numb.

They're emotionally aware.

They know what they're feeling.

They understand why they're feeling it.

And because they understand it, they're not controlled by it.

That's true emotional mastery.

Not suppression.

Awareness.

The Cost Of Numbness

Many men believe they can selectively numb emotions.

They think they can shut off pain while keeping joy.

Suppress fear while keeping courage.

Ignore grief while maintaining love.

It doesn't work like that.

Human emotions don't operate like a Spotify playlist.

You can't mute one track without affecting the entire system.

When you numb pain, you also numb joy.

When you suppress sadness, you often suppress gratitude.

When you disconnect from fear, you often disconnect from excitement.

When you close your heart to protect yourself, you also close it to connection.

The goal is not feeling less.

The goal is becoming capable of feeling more without being overwhelmed.

That's emotional strength.

Not emotional avoidance.

The Volcano

Unprocessed emotions are like pressure building inside a volcano.

For a while everything looks fine.

The mountain appears stable.

Calm.

Predictable.

Then one day it erupts.

And everyone says:

"That came out of nowhere."

No it didn't.

The pressure had been building for years.

Most emotional outbursts aren't sudden.

They're accumulated.

Accumulated resentment.

Accumulated frustration.

Accumulated grief.

Accumulated disappointment.

Accumulated fear.

Eventually the emotional debt becomes due.

And the bill is expensive.

I've seen men destroy marriages because of it.

Destroy friendships because of it.

Destroy careers because of it.

Destroy themselves because of it.

Not because they were emotional.

Because they spent years pretending they weren't.

The Emotion Behind The Emotion

One of the most powerful lessons I learned was that emotions often travel in disguise.

Anger is a great example.

Many men think they're angry.

Sometimes they are.

But often anger is simply the bodyguard.

Standing behind anger is something more vulnerable.

Fear.

Shame.

Hurt.

Rejection.

Sadness.

Disappointment.

The reason many men stay stuck is because they only deal with the bodyguard.

They never meet the person being protected.

The same is true for many emotional struggles.

What looks like frustration may actually be grief.

What looks like arrogance may actually be insecurity.

What looks like control may actually be fear.

What looks like perfectionism may actually be shame.

Until you understand what's underneath, nothing changes.

The Turning Point

One of the biggest shifts in my life happened when I stopped asking:

"How do I get rid of this feeling?"

And started asking:

"What is this feeling trying to teach me?"

That question changes everything.

Because emotions are information.

Not instructions.

Information.

Fear tells you something matters.

Anger tells you a boundary may have been crossed.

Sadness tells you something valuable was lost.

Guilt tells you something may be misaligned with your values.

Emotions are messengers.

The problem is that most men shoot the messenger before reading the message.

Then wonder why the same emotional patterns keep returning.

The Courage To Feel

The irony is that avoiding emotions actually makes them stronger.

Facing them makes them weaker.

Not immediately.

But eventually.

The emotion you've been running from for years often becomes manageable the moment you stop running.

Think about that.

The thing you feared most was never the emotion.

It was feeling the emotion.

And once you realise you can survive the feeling, its power starts disappearing.

Not because the emotion changes.

Because your relationship with it changes.

That's emotional maturity.

Not controlling your emotions.

Developing the courage to experience them.

The Elevated Man

The Elevated Man does not fear his emotional world.

He doesn't worship emotions.

He doesn't become controlled by them.

But he doesn't avoid them either.

He understands that emotions are part of being human.

Not evidence of weakness.

He can feel sadness without becoming hopeless.

Fear without becoming paralysed.

Anger without becoming destructive.

Grief without becoming broken.

Because he knows something many men never learn.

An emotion is just a visitor.

No matter how intense it feels, it eventually passes.

But only if you allow it to move through you.

What you resist persists.

What you process transforms.

The Elevated Man Challenge

For the next seven days, stop asking:

"How do I stop feeling this?"

Instead ask:

"What am I feeling?"

"What triggered it?"

"What is this emotion trying to tell me?"

"What need, value, fear, or wound might sit underneath it?"

Write your answers down.

Don't analyse.

Observe.

Don't judge.

Notice.

Most men spend years trying to escape their emotions.

The Elevated Man learns to understand them.

Because emotional mastery doesn't come from suppression.

It comes from awareness.

And awareness is where freedom begins.

The prison was never your emotions.

The prison was believing you had to escape them.

CHAPTER NINE

Good Men Feel

The strength found in emotional mastery

One of the dumbest things men have ever been taught is that emotions make us weak.

Think about that for a second.

Half of the human experience.

Half of what makes us alive.

Half of what creates connection, purpose, love, courage, passion, meaning and joy.

And somehow we've convinced ourselves it's a problem.

It's madness.

Yet millions of men still believe it.

Not consciously.

But deeply.

Emotion equals weakness.

Vulnerability equals weakness.

Sadness equals weakness.

Fear equals weakness.

Need equals weakness.

The result?

Men become emotional fugitives.

Running from their own humanity.

Trying desperately to outrun feelings that were never chasing them in the first place.

I know because I did it too.

For years.

The Strong Silent Man

Most of us grew up with some version of the same message.

Be tough.

Don't cry.

Harden up.

Man up.

Get over it.

Move on.

Now let's be fair.

There is some wisdom in resilience.

Life is hard.

Pain is inevitable.

Responsibility matters.

Nobody is coming to save you.

Those lessons have value.

The problem is what happened next.

Somewhere along the way resilience got confused with suppression.

Strength got confused with numbness.

Masculinity got confused with emotional avoidance.

And generations of men inherited a terrible belief:

"If I feel it, I shouldn't show it."

Which sounds strong.

Until you see the damage it causes.

The Men We Become

When a boy learns that certain emotions are unacceptable, he doesn't stop feeling them.

He simply learns to hide them.

Fear becomes anger.

Sadness becomes withdrawal.

Loneliness becomes workaholism.

Insecurity becomes arrogance.

Shame becomes perfectionism.

Pain becomes addiction.

The emotion never disappears.

It just changes clothes.

Then one day he becomes a man.

And he wonders why:

He feels disconnected.

His relationships struggle.

He feels misunderstood.

His marriage feels distant.

His anxiety is growing.

His anger appears unexpectedly.

His depression won't leave.

The answer is often simpler than he realises.

He's carrying years of unprocessed emotional weight.

The Lie About Masculinity

I spent years studying masculinity.

Not because I wanted to become an alpha.

Because I wanted to become a better man.

And here's what I discovered.

The strongest men I've ever met were not emotionally numb.

They were emotionally aware.

They knew exactly what they were feeling.

Exactly why they were feeling it.

And exactly what to do with it.

They weren't controlled by their emotions.

But neither were they disconnected from them.

That's real strength.

Not avoidance.

Awareness.

The world doesn't need more emotionally disconnected men.

It needs more emotionally intelligent men.

Men who can sit with discomfort.

Men who can have difficult conversations.

Men who can experience grief without collapsing.

Men who can experience fear without quitting.

Men who can experience sadness without shame.

That's strength.

Not pretending nothing hurts.

The Day Everything Changed

One of the biggest turning points in my life happened after I stopped treating emotions like enemies.

For years I approached emotional pain like something to defeat.

Conquer.

Eliminate.

Suppress.

Avoid.

Eventually I realised something.

The battle itself was exhausting me.

Imagine spending every day fighting your own mind.

Fighting your own emotions.

Fighting your own humanity.

No wonder so many men are exhausted.

No wonder so many feel disconnected.

No wonder so many feel lost.

You cannot be at war with yourself and experience peace at the same time.

Eventually I stopped asking:

"How do I stop feeling this?"

And started asking:

"What happens if I allow myself to feel it?"

That question changed everything.

What Courage Actually Looks Like

Most men think courage means fearlessness.

It doesn't.

Fearlessness is either stupidity or psychopathy.

Courage is feeling fear and moving anyway.

The same principle applies emotionally.

Emotional courage is not the absence of pain.

It's the willingness to experience pain without running.

The willingness to sit with grief.

The willingness to face shame.

The willingness to acknowledge loneliness.

The willingness to admit you're struggling.

The willingness to tell the truth.

That's courage.

Far more courage than pretending everything is fine.

Some of the bravest moments of my life weren't public.

They weren't dramatic.

They happened in quiet rooms.

Private conversations.

Difficult admissions.

Moments where I stopped hiding from myself.

Moments where I admitted I wasn't okay.

Moments where I allowed myself to feel what I'd spent years avoiding.

That's courage.

And it changed my life.

The Gift Of Grief

One emotion men particularly struggle with is grief.

Not just grief from death.

Grief from life.

The end of relationships.

Lost opportunities.

Unfulfilled dreams.

Versions of ourselves we never became.

The years we spent lost.

The mistakes we wish we could undo.

The childhood wounds we never healed.

Many men carry enormous grief.

And because they never process it, it quietly influences everything.

Their relationships.

Their confidence.

Their behaviour.

Their decisions.

Their identity.

Here's the truth.

Grief is not weakness.

Grief is evidence that something mattered.

Only people who love deeply grieve deeply.

The opposite of grief isn't strength.

It's indifference.

And indifference is far more dangerous.

What My Son Taught Me

When Marinko asked me if his brain was broken, I saw something that changed me forever.

I realised that children learn emotional relationships by watching us.

Not listening to us.

Watching us.

If I wanted my son to believe his emotions were safe, I needed to model that.

If I wanted him to understand that vulnerability wasn't weakness, I needed to demonstrate it.

If I wanted him to become emotionally intelligent, I needed to become emotionally intelligent.

Because children don't become what we tell them to become.

They become what we consistently show them.

That responsibility changed the way I viewed masculinity forever.

Not as emotional control.

As emotional leadership.

Emotional Leadership

Most men hear the word leadership and think about other people.

Teams.

Businesses.

Families.

Influence.

Authority.

The most important leadership skill you'll ever develop is leading yourself.

Especially emotionally.

Can you stay calm under pressure?

Can you regulate yourself during conflict?

Can you acknowledge your emotions without becoming consumed by them?

Can you tell the truth when it's uncomfortable?

Can you remain present during pain?

That's leadership.

Because if your emotions control you, eventually they'll control every relationship you have.

And if you're disconnected from your emotions, eventually you'll become disconnected from yourself.

Neither path leads to freedom.

The Elevated Man

The Elevated Man understands something many men spend decades learning.

Emotions are not obstacles.

They're guides.

Not always accurate.

Not always rational.

But always informative.

He doesn't suppress emotions.

He processes them.

He doesn't worship emotions.

He understands them.

He doesn't become controlled by emotions.

He develops a relationship with them.

Because he knows that every emotion contains information.

Every emotion contains wisdom.

Every emotion contains an opportunity for growth.

If he's willing to listen.

The Elevated Man Challenge

For the next week, whenever you experience a strong emotion, stop and ask:

What am I feeling?

Where do I feel it in my body?

What triggered it?

What is this emotion trying to tell me?

What am I avoiding?

What truth might this emotion be pointing toward?

Write your answers down.

Don't judge them.

Don't fix them.

Don't analyse them.

Just notice them.

Most men spend their lives trying to become stronger by feeling less.

The Elevated Man becomes stronger by developing the capacity to feel more.

More truth.

More connection.

More courage.

More compassion.

More humanity.

Because strength is not the absence of emotion.

Strength is the ability to remain fully present while experiencing it.

And that may be one of the most masculine things a man can ever learn.

CHAPTER TEN

Meeting The Shadow

Facing the man you've been hiding from

There are two versions of every man.

The man the world sees.

And the man he spends his life trying to hide.

The first version is easy to talk about.

The husband.

The father.

The provider.

The leader.

The successful guy.

The reliable guy.

The good man.

The second version?

Not so much.

The jealous man.

The angry man.

The insecure man.

The frightened man.

The selfish man.

The resentful man.

The wounded man.

The version we work tirelessly to keep hidden.

Carl Jung called this part of us the Shadow.

Not because it's evil.

Because it's unconscious.

It's the collection of traits, emotions, desires, fears, and impulses we've rejected, denied, buried, or hidden from ourselves.

And whether you realise it or not...

Your shadow is running far more of your life than you'd like to admit.

The Parts We Leave Behind

As children, we learn very quickly which parts of ourselves are acceptable.

And which aren't.

Maybe you were told:

Don't be angry.

Don't be emotional.

Don't be selfish.

Don't be weak.

Don't be needy.

Don't be loud.

Don't be difficult.

Don't be sensitive.

So what do we do?

We adapt.

We suppress.

We hide.

We disconnect.

The qualities that earn acceptance become part of our identity.

The qualities that threaten acceptance get pushed into the basement.

Over time we stop seeing them altogether.

At least consciously.

But just because something becomes unconscious doesn't mean it disappears.

It simply moves underground.

And from there it continues influencing your behaviour.

Your relationships.

Your decisions.

Your emotional reactions.

Your life.

The shadow isn't destroyed.

It's merely hidden.

The Man I Didn't Want To Be

For years I saw myself as a good man.

And to be fair, I was.

I loved my family.

I worked hard.

I cared deeply.

I tried to do the right thing.

But there were parts of myself I didn't want to acknowledge.

Resentment.

Anger.

Fear.

Neediness.

Insecurity.

The desire for validation.

The fear of rejection.

Those things didn't fit the image I had of myself.

So I ignored them.

Or at least I tried to.

The problem with ignored emotions is that they don't stay quiet.

They simply find different ways to express themselves.

The anger becomes passive aggression.

The insecurity becomes people-pleasing.

The fear becomes control.

The shame becomes perfectionism.

The resentment becomes emotional distance.

What remains hidden doesn't become harmless.

It becomes powerful.

Why Certain People Drive You Crazy

Here's a fun question.

Who annoys the hell out of you?

Seriously.

Think about it.

What kind of people trigger you?

Arrogant people?

Selfish people?

Controlling people?

Attention-seeking people?

Lazy people?

Entitled people?

Now here's the uncomfortable part.

The traits that trigger us most intensely often point toward something unresolved within ourselves.

That doesn't mean you secretly are those things.

It means those qualities have emotional charge.

And emotional charge always tells a story.

For example:

Many Nice Guys hate selfish people.

Why?

Because they've spent years suppressing their own needs.

Many people-pleasers become furious with entitled people.

Why?

Because they've spent years over-giving.

Many men judge emotional people.

Why?

Because they've spent years suppressing their own emotions.

The trigger isn't the other person.

The trigger is what they're reflecting back to you.

That's projection.

And it's one of the most powerful psychological forces in existence.

The Mirror We Hate

Projection is simple.

We see parts of ourselves in others.

Then pretend they're only theirs.

Imagine standing in front of a mirror with dirt on your face.

Instead of cleaning your face, you start scrubbing the mirror.

That's projection.

You try fixing outside what actually exists inside.

Most people spend years doing this.

Complaining about qualities they secretly struggle with themselves.

Judging traits they've disowned.

Fighting battles within other people that actually belong within themselves.

I know because I did it too.

The things that irritated me most in others often revealed something important about me.

Something unresolved.

Something uncomfortable.

Something hidden.

And usually something valuable.

The Nice Guy Shadow

One of the biggest breakthroughs in my own journey was realising that even Nice Guys have shadows.

Especially Nice Guys.

In fact, many Nice Guy behaviours are shadows disguised as virtues.

Let's look at a few examples.

People-pleasing can be hidden fear.

Over-giving can be hidden neediness.

Conflict avoidance can be hidden insecurity.

Caretaking can be hidden control.

Being endlessly understanding can sometimes be hidden resentment.

Again, these behaviours aren't bad.

The question is:

What's driving them?

Virtue driven by authenticity feels freeing.

Virtue driven by fear feels exhausting.

That's the difference.

And the difference matters.

The Shadow And The Marriage

One of the reasons relationships are such powerful teachers is that they expose our shadows faster than almost anything else.

Marriage has an incredible ability to reveal who you really are.

Not who you pretend to be.

Not who you'd like to be.

Who you actually are.

When you're tired.

Triggered.

Stressed.

Scared.

Rejected.

Hurt.

That's when the shadow appears.

Not because the relationship created it.

Because the relationship exposed it.

I learned this lesson repeatedly.

Every frustration.

Every argument.

Every emotional reaction.

Every trigger.

Contained information.

Not just about the relationship.

About me.

The question wasn't:

"What is Jana doing wrong?"

The question became:

"Why is this affecting me so strongly?"

That question changed everything.

Because it moved me from blame to ownership.

And ownership creates power.

The Dark Side Of Strength

One of the biggest mistakes men make is believing they can simply eliminate their shadow.

You can't.

The goal isn't elimination.

It's integration.

Think about courage.

Without fear, courage cannot exist.

Think about boundaries.

Without aggression, boundaries cannot exist.

Think about leadership.

Without assertiveness, leadership cannot exist.

Many men reject important parts of themselves because they fear becoming toxic.

They reject anger.

Aggression.

Power.

Authority.

Assertiveness.

Dominance.

The problem is that rejected power doesn't disappear.

It often returns in unhealthy ways.

Passive aggression.

Bitterness.

Resentment.

Manipulation.

Victimhood.

The Elevated Man does not fear his power.

He learns to master it.

Because power integrated becomes leadership.

Power suppressed becomes dysfunction.

The Monster Under The Bed

When I was a kid, I thought there was a monster under my bed.

Every child knows this feeling.

You lie awake imagining all kinds of terrifying possibilities.

Then eventually you gather the courage to look.

And discover nothing's there.

The shadow works similarly.

The parts of ourselves we fear most often lose their power the moment we examine them honestly.

The anger.

The shame.

The insecurity.

The fear.

The grief.

The jealousy.

The loneliness.

They're rarely as terrifying as we imagine.

But avoiding them gives them power.

Facing them takes it away.

That's why awareness is transformational.

Not because awareness fixes everything.

Because awareness makes unconscious patterns conscious.

And once something becomes conscious, you can work with it.

The Elevated Man

The Elevated Man understands that growth requires honesty.

Brutal honesty.

Not just about his strengths.

About his weaknesses.

His wounds.

His fears.

His patterns.

His blind spots.

His shadow.

He doesn't pretend to be perfect.

He doesn't need to.

Because maturity isn't perfection.

It's integration.

The Elevated Man can acknowledge:

I am capable of anger.

I am capable of fear.

I am capable of selfishness.

I am capable of mistakes.

I am capable of failure.

And because he acknowledges those realities, they no longer control him.

The parts of ourselves we own become manageable.

The parts we deny become dangerous.

The Elevated Man Challenge

Take out a notebook and answer these questions:

Who triggers me most?

What specific qualities trigger me?

When have I displayed those same qualities?

What emotions do I judge most harshly in others?

What emotions do I avoid most in myself?

What parts of myself am I afraid people would discover?

What strengths have I been suppressing because I fear how others might react?

Then answer this final question:

What if the thing I'm avoiding contains the very lesson I need most?

Sit with that.

Because the next level of your growth will not come from discovering new strengths.

It will come from integrating the parts of yourself you've spent years trying to hide.

The shadow is not your enemy.

The shadow is the doorway.

And on the other side of that doorway is something every man is searching for, wholeness.

PART IV
STRENGTH OF CHARACTER
Becoming The Man You Respect

CHAPTER ELEVEN

Boundaries: Self-Respect In Action

The line between love and self-abandonment

If I could teach every man one skill, it wouldn't be confidence.

It wouldn't be communication.

It wouldn't be leadership.

It wouldn't even be discipline.

It would be boundaries.

Because almost every problem I've ever seen in men's lives can be traced back to one issue:

A lack of self-respect.

And nowhere is self-respect more visible than in the boundaries you allow people to cross.

Think about it.

Every resentment you've ever carried.

Every relationship that drained you.

Every situation where you felt used.

Every time you felt taken for granted.

Every moment you felt trapped.

Every occasion where you silently thought:

"This isn't okay."

But did nothing.

At the centre of all those experiences was usually the same problem.

A boundary that wasn't communicated.

Or a boundary that wasn't enforced.

Most men don't have a boundary problem.

They have a self-worth problem.

Because boundaries are not walls.

They're self-respect in action.

The Word That Changed My Life

For years there was one word I struggled to use.

No.

Such a tiny word.

Two letters.

One syllable.

Yet for many men it's one of the hardest words in the English language.

Especially Nice Guys.

Especially people-pleasers.

Especially men whose identity has been built around being helpful, needed, agreeable, and dependable.

Saying yes feels natural.

Saying no feels selfish.

At least that's what we tell ourselves.

The problem is that every time you say yes when you really mean no, something important happens.

You betray yourself.

And your subconscious notices.

Every single time.

You may convince everyone else.

You won't convince yourself.

That's why many men feel exhausted.

They're carrying the weight of a thousand tiny betrayals.

Every unwanted commitment.

Every unspoken frustration.

Every suppressed opinion.

Every tolerated disrespect.

Every fake smile.

Every forced agreement.

Every unnecessary yes.

Self-respect slowly leaks away.

Not through major events.

Through daily compromises.

The Cost Of Keeping The Peace

For most of my life, I believed keeping the peace was a virtue.

Avoid conflict.

Stay calm.

Be understanding.

Be accommodating.

Be patient.

Be reasonable.

Again, none of those things are bad.

The problem is that many men confuse peacekeeping with self-abandonment.

There's a difference.

A massive difference.

One comes from maturity.

The other comes from fear.

Peacekeeping asks:

"How do we solve this?"

Self-abandonment asks:

"How do I avoid discomfort?"

Many men spend years avoiding difficult conversations because they fear conflict.

But conflict avoided rarely disappears.

It simply transforms.

Into resentment.

Into frustration.

Into distance.

Into passive aggression.

Into emotional disconnection.

Eventually the conflict arrives anyway.

Only now it's bigger.

And more painful.

Because it has years of accumulated weight behind it.

The Marriage Test

One of the places boundaries matter most is marriage.

Not because marriage creates boundary problems.

Because marriage exposes them.

Many men enter relationships believing love means endless sacrifice.

I certainly did.

The thinking goes something like this:

If I love her, I'll put her first.

If I love her, I'll compromise.

If I love her, I'll make her happy.

Again, sounds noble.

Until it becomes your entire identity.

Then something strange happens.

You stop expressing preferences.

You stop voicing needs.

You stop advocating for yourself.

You stop being honest.

Not because you don't care.

Because you're afraid honesty might create tension.

But here's what I learned.

Honesty creates intimacy.

Not agreement.

Intimacy.

You cannot be deeply connected to someone while hiding parts of yourself.

The strongest relationships aren't built on constant harmony.

They're built on truth.

And truth requires boundaries.

Why Men Fear Boundaries

Most men fear boundaries for one reason.

Rejection.

We tell ourselves stories.

If I say no, they'll be upset.

If I set a boundary, they'll leave.

If I speak up, they'll think I'm selfish.

If I disappoint them, they'll stop loving me.

These fears often trace all the way back to childhood.

Back to approval.

Back to belonging.

Back to worthiness.

The child learned:

Connection requires compliance.

The adult continues acting accordingly.

But here's the truth.

Relationships that require self-abandonment to survive are not healthy relationships.

Healthy people respect healthy boundaries.

Unhealthy people often resist them.

That's why boundaries reveal so much.

They show you who respects you.

And who only benefited from your lack of self-respect.

The Difference Between Nice And Kind

One of the biggest breakthroughs in my life was learning the difference between being nice and being kind.

Most people think they're the same thing.

They're not.

Nice avoids discomfort.

Kind embraces truth.

Nice says yes when it wants to say no.

Kind says no when it's necessary.

Nice seeks approval.

Kind seeks integrity.

Nice prioritises harmony.

Kind prioritises honesty.

Nice often comes from fear.

Kind comes from courage.

This distinction changed everything for me.

Because I realised many of my so-called nice behaviours weren't actually acts of kindness.

They were attempts to avoid discomfort.

And avoiding discomfort is not a virtue.

It's a survival strategy.

The Boundary Revolution

Everything changed when I stopped asking:

"Will they like this?"

And started asking:

"Does this honour my values?"

That single question transformed my decision-making.

Because boundaries aren't about controlling others.

They're about controlling access to you.

You don't control what people say.

You don't control what people do.

You don't control how people respond.

You only control what you allow.

That's your responsibility.

Not theirs.

Yours.

The moment you understand that, your life changes.

Because you stop waiting for others to respect you.

You start respecting yourself.

And people respond accordingly.

Boundaries Create Freedom

Most people think boundaries restrict freedom.

The opposite is true.

Boundaries create freedom.

Think about a football field.

Without boundaries, there is no game.

Without rules, there is chaos.

Without structure, there is confusion.

The same applies to life.

Boundaries create clarity.

Clarity creates trust.

Trust creates safety.

Safety creates connection.

The strongest relationships I've ever seen have clear boundaries.

The healthiest workplaces have clear boundaries.

The healthiest friendships have clear boundaries.

The healthiest people have clear boundaries.

Because boundaries are not barriers to connection.

They are the foundation of connection.

The Hardest Boundary

The hardest boundary I ever learned wasn't with other people.

It was with myself.

Because self-respect begins internally.

It means:

Keeping your word.

Following through.

Honouring commitments.

Living your values.

Maintaining your standards.

Not negotiating with excuses.

Many men demand respect from others while constantly disrespecting themselves.

They break promises to themselves.

Ignore their values.

Abandon their standards.

Then wonder why confidence feels fragile.

Confidence is self-trust.

Self-trust is built through integrity.

Integrity begins with the promises you make to yourself.

The first boundary every man must learn is this:

I will no longer betray myself.

Everything else grows from there.

The Elevated Man

The Elevated Man understands that boundaries are not aggressive.

They're not selfish.

They're not controlling.

They're not unkind.

They're expressions of self-respect.

He understands that every yes means no to something else.

So he chooses carefully.

He understands that discomfort is often the price of authenticity.

So he tells the truth anyway.

He understands that not everyone will like his boundaries.

So he stops needing everyone to like him.

Most importantly, he understands that boundaries protect the things that matter most.

His values.

His time.

His energy.

His family.

His mission.

His peace.

Because what you fail to protect eventually disappears.

The Elevated Man Challenge

For the next seven days, pay attention to every situation where you feel:

Resentful.

Frustrated.

Drained.

Taken for granted.

Disrespected.

Then ask yourself:

What boundary was missing?

What truth did I avoid expressing?

What did I say yes to when I wanted to say no?

What discomfort was I trying to avoid?

Now choose one small boundary.

One conversation.

One honest statement.

One respectful no.

Nothing dramatic.

Just one act of self-respect.

Then pay attention to what happens.

Because most men spend their lives waiting for confidence before they set boundaries.

The Elevated Man learns something different.

Confidence doesn't create boundaries.

Boundaries create confidence.

Every time you honour yourself, self-trust grows.

Every time self-trust grows, confidence follows.

And confidence built on self-respect is something no one can take away.

Because it's no longer dependent on their approval.

It's built on your integrity.

And integrity is where real strength lives.

CHAPTER TWELVE

The Invisible Prison

How fear quietly controls your decisions

Most men think fear looks like cowardice.

It doesn't.

Fear is much smarter than that.

If fear looked like a trembling man hiding under a bed, we'd all recognise it immediately.

The problem is that fear wears disguises.

It shows up as procrastination.

Perfectionism.

People-pleasing.

Overthinking.

Control.

Avoidance.

Indecision.

Workaholism.

Comfort.

Excuses.

Fear rarely announces itself.

It whispers.

And if you're not paying attention, you'll spend your entire life obeying it without ever realising who's giving the orders.

I know because that's exactly what I did.

For years.

The Most Powerful Force In Your Life

Take a moment and think about the biggest regrets in your life.

The opportunities you didn't take.

The conversations you didn't have.

The boundaries you didn't set.

The risks you avoided.

The dreams you abandoned.

The truth you never spoke.

Now ask yourself:

How many of those decisions were actually caused by fear?

Most.

Maybe all.

That's because fear is one of the most powerful forces in human behaviour.

Not because it's bad.

Because it's designed to keep us alive.

Thousands of years ago, fear kept our ancestors from becoming lunch.

Fear said:

Don't touch that snake.

Don't walk off that cliff.

Don't wander into the dark forest.

Useful.

Very useful.

The problem is that your brain still uses the same survival software today.

The only difference is that modern threats aren't usually physical.

They're emotional.

Rejection.

Failure.

Embarrassment.

Judgement.

Criticism.

Disappointment.

Abandonment.

And your brain reacts to those threats as if they're life-threatening.

Which means many men spend their lives trying to survive situations that aren't actually dangerous.

The Four Fear Responses

Most people know about fight or flight.

Few understand the full picture.

When fear appears, humans generally respond in four ways.

Fight.

Flight.

Freeze.

Appease.

Let's break them down.

Fight says:

Attack the threat.

Flight says:

Avoid the threat.

Freeze says:

Do nothing.

Appease says:

Keep everyone happy.

The first three are widely understood.

The fourth one changes lives once you recognise it.

Because many Nice Guys aren't operating from kindness.

They're operating from appeasement.

They're trying to stay safe.

Emotionally safe.

Relationally safe.

Psychologically safe.

And once you understand that, everything starts making sense.

The Appeaser

The appeaser is terrified of conflict.

Terrified of rejection.

Terrified of disappointing people.

Terrified of being misunderstood.

Terrified of upsetting someone.

So he adapts.

Agrees.

Accommodates.

Compromises.

Sacrifices.

Not because he wants to.

Because fear tells him it's necessary.

Fear says:

If they're upset, you're unsafe.

If they reject you, you're unsafe.

If they leave, you're unsafe.

If they disapprove, you're unsafe.

The appeaser's entire life becomes a strategy for avoiding discomfort.

The tragedy is that it works.

At first.

People like him.

He's agreeable.

Easy-going.

Helpful.

Generous.

Until eventually he becomes exhausted.

Resentful.

Invisible.

Disconnected.

Because the cost of appeasement is always authenticity.

You cannot be yourself while constantly managing everyone else's emotions.

My Prison Had No Bars

Looking back, one of the most uncomfortable realisations of my life was understanding how many of my decisions had been fear-based.

Not because I was weak.

Because I was human.

Many of the things I called responsibility were actually fear.

Many of the things I called patience were actually fear.

Many of the things I called understanding were actually fear.

Fear of conflict.

Fear of rejection.

Fear of losing people.

Fear of not being enough.

Fear of failure.

Fear of judgement.

The prison I lived inside didn't have bars.

It had beliefs.

And beliefs are much harder to see.

Because when you've lived with them your entire life, they feel like reality.

Not fear.

Reality.

That's why personal growth often feels so uncomfortable.

You're not just changing behaviour.

You're challenging beliefs you've mistaken for truth.

Fear's Favourite Question

Fear loves one question more than any other.

What if?

What if I fail?

What if they reject me?

What if they get angry?

What if I embarrass myself?

What if it doesn't work?

What if I lose everything?

Fear lives in imagined futures.

It feeds on uncertainty.

And because the future doesn't exist yet, fear gets to make up whatever story it wants.

Here's what's interesting.

Most people never challenge fear's questions.

They simply obey them.

But what if we asked a different question?

What if it works?

What if this conversation improves the relationship?

What if setting the boundary earns respect?

What if starting the business changes your life?

What if telling the truth creates freedom?

What if the thing you're avoiding contains exactly what you need?

Fear hates those questions.

Because fear thrives when possibilities are ignored.

The Price Of Safety

One of the most dangerous things fear offers is comfort.

Comfort feels safe.

Comfort feels familiar.

Comfort feels predictable.

The problem is that comfort quietly steals your future.

Every meaningful thing in my life required discomfort.

Approaching Jana.

Getting married.

Becoming a father.

Facing depression.

Joining the Alpha Code.

Having difficult conversations.

Setting boundaries.

Changing my identity.

Every single one required discomfort.

Growth always does.

Which means the question isn't:

Can I avoid discomfort?

The question is:

Which discomfort am I willing to choose?

Because every path contains discomfort.

The discomfort of growth.

Or the discomfort of regret.

Choose carefully.

One creates expansion.

The other creates suffering.

Courage Is Not Confidence

Many men believe they need confidence before they act.

That's backwards.

Confidence comes after action.

Courage comes before it.

Think about the bravest thing you've ever done.

Were you confident beforehand?

Probably not.

You were scared.

Terrified even.

But you acted anyway.

That's courage.

And courage creates evidence.

Evidence creates confidence.

Confidence is not the cause.

It's the result.

This was one of the biggest lessons of my transformation.

I spent years waiting to feel ready.

Then I realised readiness is a myth.

The men you admire aren't fearless.

They've simply developed a different relationship with fear.

Fear And The Elevated Man

The Elevated Man still feels fear.

Every single one of them does.

The difference is that he no longer worships it.

He listens to it.

Considers it.

Then decides for himself.

Fear gets a vote.

It doesn't get a veto.

That's leadership.

Self-leadership.

Fear says:

Don't speak up.

He speaks anyway.

Fear says:

Don't set the boundary.

He sets it anyway.

Fear says:

Don't take the risk.

He moves anyway.

Fear says:

Stay where it's safe.

He grows anyway.

Not because he's fearless.

Because he's committed to something bigger than fear.

His values.

His mission.

His integrity.

His future.

The Cemetery Of Potential

One of the saddest places in the world isn't a prison.

It's not a hospital.

It's not a cemetery.

It's the space inside a man who never became who he was capable of becoming.

A man who spent his entire life obeying fear.

The business never started.

The truth never spoken.

The boundary never set.

The dream never pursued.

The life never lived.

The potential remains buried.

Not because he lacked talent.

Not because he lacked opportunity.

Because fear convinced him to stay safe.

And safety became his prison.

I don't want that for you.

I don't want that for my son.

I don't want that for any man reading this book.

The Elevated Man Challenge

Make a list of five things you're currently avoiding.

Conversations.

Decisions.

Risks.

Boundaries.

Opportunities.

Anything.

Now write down the fear underneath each one.

Be honest.

Not the excuse.

The fear.

Then answer this question:

If I knew I couldn't fail, what would I do?

Finally, choose one item.

Just one.

And take one uncomfortable action within the next 24 hours.

Not next week.

Not next month.

Today.

Because courage is built exactly the same way strength is built.

One repetition at a time.

One uncomfortable action at a time.

One act of courage at a time.

Most men spend their lives waiting for fear to disappear.

The Elevated Man learns something different.

Fear never disappears.

But it does become smaller.

Smaller every time you walk through it.

Smaller every time you tell the truth.

Smaller every time you honour your values.

Smaller every time you refuse to let it make your decisions.

Eventually you realise something profound.

The prison door was never locked.

Fear simply convinced you it was.

And the moment you take responsibility for your life, you discover what was true all along.

You were never trapped.

You were just afraid to leave.

CHAPTER THIRTEEN

The Courage To Be Disliked

Freedom from the need for approval

For most of my life, I wanted people to like me.

Actually, that's not entirely true.

I needed people to like me.

There's a difference.

Wanting approval is human.

Needing approval is a prison.

And for many years, I lived inside that prison without even knowing it existed.

I thought I was being kind.

I thought I was being considerate.

I thought I was being a good husband.

A good father.

A good friend.

A good bloke.

The truth was far less flattering.

Much of my behaviour was being driven by a single fear.

What if they don't like me?

That question controlled more of my life than I ever realised.

And if you're honest, there's a good chance it's controlling more of yours than you'd like to admit.

The Human Condition

Let's get something clear.

Wanting acceptance is normal.

We're tribal creatures.

For most of human history, rejection from the tribe meant death.

If the group abandoned you, you didn't survive.

Your nervous system still carries that ancient programming.

Which is why criticism hurts.

Which is why rejection stings.

Which is why disapproval feels uncomfortable.

Your brain interprets social rejection as danger.

The problem isn't that we feel that discomfort.

The problem is when we allow it to dictate our lives.

That's where things go wrong.

Because eventually we stop asking:

"What is true?"

And start asking:

"What will keep people happy?"

One question creates freedom.

The other creates performance.

The Impossible Mission

There is a mission many men spend their entire lives trying to accomplish.

It's impossible.

And it goes something like this:

Make everybody happy.

Be liked by everyone.

Avoid criticism.

Avoid conflict.

Avoid rejection.

Avoid judgement.

Avoid disappointment.

Avoid upsetting people.

Good luck.

It's impossible.

Not difficult.

Impossible.

You could become the most generous man alive.

Someone will think you're weak.

You could become incredibly successful.

Someone will think you're arrogant.

You could become deeply compassionate.

Someone will think you're soft.

You could become fiercely disciplined.

Someone will think you're obsessed.

No matter what you do, somebody will disagree.

That's not a flaw in life.

That's life.

The moment you understand this, something remarkable happens.

You stop trying to win a game that was never designed to be won.

The Day I Stopped Chasing Approval

One of the biggest breakthroughs in my life wasn't learning how to gain approval.

It was learning how to survive without it.

That sounds simple.

It's not.

For a man who has spent decades measuring his value through acceptance, it's revolutionary.

Because approval addiction creates a dangerous pattern.

You become emotionally dependent on other people's opinions.

If they approve, you feel good.

If they disapprove, you feel terrible.

Your emotional state becomes outsourced.

Your self-worth becomes outsourced.

Your identity becomes outsourced.

And eventually your life becomes outsourced.

You no longer belong to yourself.

You belong to public opinion.

That's not freedom.

That's emotional servitude.

The day I realised this was the day everything began to change.

Why Nice Guys Stay Stuck

Most Nice Guys don't lack courage.

They misdirect it.

They'll work long hours.

Carry enormous responsibility.

Sacrifice for their families.

Push through exhaustion.

Endure hardship.

But ask them to disappoint someone?

Terrifying.

Ask them to say no?

Terrifying.

Ask them to express an unpopular opinion?

Terrifying.

Ask them to prioritise their own needs occasionally?

Terrifying.

Why?

Because many Nice Guys aren't afraid of conflict.

They're afraid of rejection.

And rejection threatens the thing they've built their identity around.

Approval.

That's why people-pleasing feels so difficult to overcome.

It's not a behavioural issue.

It's an identity issue.

The Truth About Rejection

One of the most liberating truths I've ever learned is this:

Rejection is information.

Not condemnation.

Someone rejecting you doesn't automatically mean you're wrong.

It doesn't mean you're unworthy.

It doesn't mean you're broken.

It simply means there's a mismatch somewhere.

Values.

Preferences.

Expectations.

Timing.

Compatibility.

Perspective.

That's all.

Yet many men interpret rejection as proof of inadequacy.

Which explains why they spend so much energy trying to avoid it.

Here's the irony.

The more you fear rejection, the more control it has over your life.

The less you fear rejection, the freer you become.

Not because rejection stops happening.

Because it stops defining you.

The Cost Of Being Liked

Everything in life has a price.

Success has a price.

Growth has a price.

Leadership has a price.

Authenticity has a price.

Being liked has a price too.

And for many men, that price is far too high.

The price is honesty.

The price is boundaries.

The price is authenticity.

The price is self-respect.

The price is truth.

The price is identity.

Many men spend decades paying that price.

Until one day they wake up exhausted.

Disconnected.

Resentful.

Wondering why they feel invisible.

The answer is simple.

They traded themselves for approval.

And approval is never worth that exchange.

The Man Jana Fell In Love With

Something occurred to me during my own journey.

The version of me that Jana fell in love with wasn't desperately trying to be liked.

The young bloke who threw his phone number out a car window wasn't calculating public opinion.

He wasn't managing perceptions.

He wasn't asking for permission.

He was simply being himself.

Fearless?

Not even close.

Terrified, actually.

But authentic.

That's what made him attractive.

Not perfection.

Authenticity.

Somewhere along the way, many men forget this.

They believe becoming more acceptable makes them more attractive.

It often does the opposite.

Because authenticity is magnetic.

People can feel it.

The same applies to leadership.

Friendship.

Marriage.

Fatherhood.

People don't connect with perfection.

They connect with truth.

The Freedom Of Authenticity

The moment you stop needing everyone to like you, something strange happens.

You become easier to like.

Not because you're trying harder.

Because you're finally real.

You stop performing.

You stop editing.

You stop filtering.

You stop managing perceptions.

You stop pretending.

You become authentic.

And authenticity creates connection.

Not universal connection.

Real connection.

The kind built on truth.

Some people will dislike it.

Good.

That's how you know it's genuine.

Because if everyone likes you, you're probably hiding something.

Usually yourself.

The Legacy Question

One day you'll be gone.

I know that's not the most uplifting sentence in the world.

But it's true.

One day people will tell stories about you.

Your wife.

Your children.

Your friends.

Your grandchildren.

What story do you want them telling?

Do you want them saying:

"He was liked by everyone."

Or:

"He lived with courage."

"He stood for something."

"He was authentic."

"He told the truth."

"He honoured his values."

"He was unapologetically himself."

One legacy requires approval.

The other requires courage.

Choose carefully.

Because one creates comfort.

The other creates meaning.

The Elevated Man

The Elevated Man understands a truth that changes everything.

He is not responsible for managing everyone's emotions.

He is not responsible for everyone's happiness.

He is not responsible for everyone's opinions.

He is not responsible for universal approval.

He is responsible for one thing.

Living with integrity.

That's it.

He tells the truth.

He honours his values.

He respects others.

He respects himself.

He communicates clearly.

He accepts responsibility.

And then he lets people decide what they think.

Because he understands something many men never learn.

Being disliked is not the opposite of being loved.

Being fake is.

The moment you become authentic, some people will disapprove.

That's inevitable.

The moment you stop needing their approval, freedom begins.

That's transformational.

The Elevated Man Challenge

Write down the names of five people whose opinions significantly influence your behaviour.

Then answer these questions:

What am I afraid would happen if they disapproved of me?

What truth have I been withholding to maintain their approval?

What boundaries have I avoided setting?

What decisions am I making for them rather than for me?

Now answer one final question:

If I was no longer afraid of being disliked, what would I do differently starting today?

Write down your answer.

Then act on it.

One action.

One conversation.

One boundary.

One truth.

Because courage is not the absence of fear.

And authenticity is not the absence of rejection.

The Elevated Man understands both.

He simply refuses to sacrifice himself in exchange for acceptance.

Because the cost is too high.

And because life becomes infinitely more meaningful the moment you stop asking:

"How do I get everyone to like me?"

And start asking:

"How do I become the man I respect?"

Answer that question honestly.

And you'll never need another person's permission to be yourself again.

PART V
THE ELEVATED MAN
Becoming The Man You Respect

CHAPTER FOURTEEN

Love Without Losing Yourself

Facing the man you've been hiding from

For a long time, I thought love meant sacrifice.

The more you loved someone, the more you sacrificed.

Simple.

Logical.

Wrong.

Now before you grab your pitchfork and accuse me of becoming selfish, let me explain.

Love absolutely requires sacrifice.

Marriage requires sacrifice.

Fatherhood requires sacrifice.

Relationships require sacrifice.

But sacrifice and self-abandonment are not the same thing.

One comes from love.

The other comes from fear.

One strengthens relationships.

The other slowly destroys them.

And for years, I didn't understand the difference.

The Fairytale Nobody Questions

Most of us grow up believing a version of the same story.

You find the right person.

You fall in love.

You give them your heart.

You become one.

Sounds beautiful.

And it is.

Until people start interpreting "becoming one" as losing themselves.

That's where the trouble begins.

Because many men unconsciously enter relationships believing their role is to become whatever their partner needs.

The provider.

The protector.

The fixer.

The problem solver.

The peacekeeper.

The emotional shock absorber.

And over time, they begin shaping themselves around the relationship.

Not maliciously.

Not consciously.

Gradually.

One compromise at a time.

One silence at a time.

One unspoken truth at a time.

Until eventually they wake up and realise something disturbing.

They've become a stranger to themselves.

The Relationship Trap

One of the biggest mistakes men make is expecting a relationship to provide what only identity can provide.

Worth.

Purpose.

Direction.

Self-respect.

Certainty.

Security.

When those things are missing internally, we often go searching for them externally.

Usually through love.

The problem is that relationships were never designed to carry that weight.

Your partner cannot provide your identity.

Your partner cannot provide your self-worth.

Your partner cannot provide your purpose.

They can support those things.

Encourage those things.

Celebrate those things.

But they cannot create them.

That's your job.

And when we ask relationships to do work they were never designed to do, both people suffer.

The Man Jana Needed

One of the most confronting lessons I learned during my own journey was this:

Jana didn't need a man who constantly sacrificed himself.

She needed a man who knew who he was.

Think about that.

For years I thought being a good husband meant giving more.

Trying harder.

Sacrificing more.

Being more available.

Being more understanding.

The irony is that none of those things were the real issue.

The issue was that somewhere along the way I had become disconnected from myself.

And when a man loses himself, everyone around him feels it.

His confidence changes.

His energy changes.

His leadership changes.

His presence changes.

His certainty changes.

The relationship feels it.

The family feels it.

The children feel it.

Because people don't just respond to what you do.

They respond to who you're being.

And I wasn't fully being myself.

I was performing.

Managing.

Pleasing.

Adapting.

Trying to avoid discomfort.

Trying to avoid rejection.

Trying to avoid conflict.

Trying to avoid disappointment.

None of which creates intimacy.

Why Honesty Creates Love

One of the greatest myths about relationships is that agreement creates connection.

It doesn't.

Honesty creates connection.

You can agree with someone every day for twenty years and still feel disconnected.

You can disagree with someone regularly and feel deeply connected.

Why?

Because intimacy requires truth.

Not perfection.

Truth.

When you hide your opinions, intimacy suffers.

When you suppress your needs, intimacy suffers.

When you avoid difficult conversations, intimacy suffers.

When you become who you think your partner wants you to be, intimacy suffers.

Because connection only occurs when the real you is present.

Not the edited version.

Not the filtered version.

The real version.

That's why authenticity is one of the most loving things you can bring into a relationship.

Even when it's uncomfortable.

Especially when it's uncomfortable.

The Fear Of Losing Love

Most people don't lose themselves because they're weak.

They lose themselves because they're afraid.

Afraid of conflict.

Afraid of rejection.

Afraid of abandonment.

Afraid of not being enough.

Afraid of losing the relationship.

I understand that fear.

I've lived that fear.

But here's what I eventually learned.

The moment you abandon yourself to keep a relationship, you've already lost something important.

Yourself.

And a relationship built on self-abandonment is never truly secure.

Because deep down you know the connection is conditional.

It's dependent on your performance.

Your compliance.

Your adaptation.

Your sacrifice.

That's not intimacy.

That's emotional negotiation.

Real love doesn't require you to disappear.

It requires you to show up.

The Strongest Version Of Love

As my marriage evolved, my understanding of love evolved too.

I stopped seeing love as self-sacrifice.

I started seeing love as self-expression.

Not selfish expression.

Authentic expression.

The strongest version of love isn't:

"I'll become whoever you need me to be."

The strongest version of love is:

"I'll bring my full self into this relationship."

My strengths.

My flaws.

My needs.

My boundaries.

My dreams.

My fears.

My truth.

Because that's what creates intimacy.

Not performance.

Presence.

And presence requires authenticity.

What Marinko Taught Me About Love

Becoming a father changed everything.

Not just because I loved my son.

Because he forced me to examine the example I was setting.

Children don't learn relationships from books.

They learn them from observation.

Every day Marinko watches how I treat Jana.

How I treat myself.

How I handle conflict.

How I communicate.

How I set boundaries.

How I express emotions.

How I show love.

Whether I realise it or not, I'm teaching him what relationships look like.

And one day he'll carry those lessons into his own relationships.

That responsibility humbled me.

Because I realised something.

I don't want my son growing up believing love requires self-abandonment.

I want him to understand that love and authenticity can coexist.

That commitment and individuality can coexist.

That connection and self-respect can coexist.

Because they must.

The Relationship Most Men Ignore

The most important relationship in your life isn't your marriage.

It isn't your friendships.

It isn't even your relationship with your children.

It's your relationship with yourself.

Because every other relationship is filtered through it.

If you don't trust yourself, relationships suffer.

If you don't respect yourself, relationships suffer.

If you don't know yourself, relationships suffer.

If you don't value yourself, relationships suffer.

The relationship with yourself sets the standard for every other relationship you experience.

Which means learning to love yourself isn't selfish.

It's foundational.

Without it, everything else becomes unstable.

Love Without Fear

One of the most beautiful things that happened during my transformation was that love became simpler.

Not easier.

Simpler.

I stopped trying to earn it.

I stopped trying to control it.

I stopped trying to secure it through performance.

I stopped trying to deserve it.

I simply allowed it.

And something surprising happened.

The less I needed love to prove my worth, the more freely I could give it.

The less I needed Jana's approval, the more deeply I could appreciate her.

The less I relied on the relationship for identity, the stronger the relationship became.

Because love thrives in freedom.

Not dependency.

The Elevated Man

The Elevated Man loves deeply.

Perhaps deeper than most.

But he does not lose himself in the process.

He knows who he is.

He knows what he values.

He knows what he stands for.

He knows what he needs.

He knows what he will and will not tolerate.

And because of that clarity, he can love without attachment.

Give without expectation.

Commit without control.

Lead without domination.

Support without rescuing.

Protect without possessing.

His love is not built on fear.

It's built on freedom.

And freedom creates intimacy.

The Elevated Man Challenge

Answer the following questions honestly:

Where have I been abandoning myself in my relationships?

What truths have I been afraid to express?

What needs have I been suppressing?

What boundaries have I avoided setting?

What am I expecting my partner to provide that I should be providing for myself?

Now answer one final question:

If I fully respected myself, how would I show up differently in my relationships?

Write down your answer.

Then choose one action.

One conversation.

One truth.

One boundary.

One act of authenticity.

Because healthy relationships are not built when two people lose themselves in each other.

They're built when two whole people choose each other.

Every day.

Not from fear.

Not from need.

Not from dependency.

From love.

And that's one of the most powerful choices a man can ever make.

CHAPTER FIFTEEN

Masculine Leadership

The Difference Between Being Needed and Being Followed

When most people hear the word leadership, they imagine someone standing at the front of a room.

A CEO.

A coach.

A politician.

A military commander.

Someone giving orders.

Someone directing people.

Someone in charge.

For years, I thought leadership looked something like that too.

Then life taught me something different.

The most important leadership you'll ever demonstrate isn't leadership of others.

It's leadership of yourself.

Because if you can't lead yourself, eventually life will.

And life is a brutal leader.

It will push you wherever your fears push you.

Wherever your habits push you.

Wherever your emotions push you.

Wherever your excuses push you.

Self-leadership is the foundation of every other kind of leadership.

Marriage.

Fatherhood.

Business.

Friendships.

Community.

Everything begins there.

And unfortunately, most men never learn how to do it.

The Problem With Modern Masculinity

Modern men are caught between two terrible definitions of masculinity.

On one side, we have the outdated version.

The emotionally disconnected man.

The dominant man.

The controlling man.

The man who never shows vulnerability.

The man who believes strength means emotional suppression.

The man who confuses authority with leadership.

On the other side, we have a different problem.

The passive man.

The indecisive man.

The approval-seeking man.

The man who avoids responsibility.

The man who lacks direction.

The man who constantly seeks permission.

Neither version works.

One creates fear.

The other creates weakness.

And neither creates respect.

The Elevated Man rejects both.

Because masculinity was never supposed to be about domination.

It was supposed to be about responsibility.

The Moment Everything Changed

One of the biggest lessons I learned during my journey was this:

Leadership begins the moment you stop blaming.

Not because other people never contribute to problems.

They do.

Not because life is always fair.

It isn't.

But because blame gives away power.

Responsibility creates it.

For years, I looked outside myself for explanations.

My circumstances.

My stress.

My relationships.

My struggles.

My challenges.

Eventually I realised something uncomfortable.

Even when life wasn't my fault, it was still my responsibility.

Read that again.

Even when life wasn't my fault, it was still my responsibility.

That single idea changed everything.

Because responsibility transforms victims into leaders.

Leadership Is Visibility

Whether you realise it or not, people are watching you.

Your children.

Your partner.

Your friends.

Your colleagues.

Your family.

Especially your children.

One of the things fatherhood taught me is that leadership is not something you turn on.

You're leading all the time.

Through your actions.

Through your reactions.

Through your habits.

Through your standards.

Through your integrity.

Through your example.

Every day, Marinko is learning what it means to be a man by watching me.

Not listening to me.

Watching me.

How I respond to adversity.

How I treat his mother.

How I speak to people.

How I handle mistakes.

How I regulate emotions.

How I lead myself.

That responsibility is both terrifying and beautiful.

Because it reminds me that leadership isn't about perfection.

It's about example.

The Leadership Crisis

Many men today feel lost because they lack direction.

Not intelligence.

Not capability.

Direction.

And without direction, leadership becomes impossible.

You cannot lead others somewhere you're unwilling to go yourself.

You cannot create certainty for your family while living in constant uncertainty.

You cannot inspire courage while living inside fear.

You cannot teach discipline while negotiating with your own excuses.

The hardest person you'll ever lead is yourself.

That's why self-leadership matters so much.

Because once you can lead yourself, everything else becomes possible.

Not easy.

Possible.

The Myth Of Confidence

One of the biggest misconceptions about leadership is that leaders are naturally confident.

They're not.

Leadership isn't confidence.

Leadership is commitment.

Think about the people you admire most.

Are they fearless?

Probably not.

Do they always know what they're doing?

Definitely not.

What separates them is their willingness to move forward despite uncertainty.

Leadership isn't certainty.

Leadership is movement.

It's taking responsibility when others avoid it.

It's making decisions when others hesitate.

It's speaking truth when others stay silent.

It's acting according to values rather than emotions.

That's leadership.

And it's available to every man.

Leadership In Marriage

One of the most misunderstood concepts in modern relationships is masculine leadership.

Many people hear the phrase and immediately think control.

Authority.

Dominance.

That's not leadership.

That's insecurity wearing a costume.

Real leadership in marriage looks different.

It's emotional stability.

Integrity.

Presence.

Direction.

Ownership.

Honesty.

It means being willing to have difficult conversations.

Being willing to admit mistakes.

Being willing to set standards.

Being willing to take responsibility.

Being willing to grow.

It means creating emotional safety through strength.

Not through control.

Jana never needed a dictator.

She needed a partner.

A grounded man.

A present man.

A man willing to lead himself.

Because when a man leads himself effectively, leadership naturally appears in every area of his life.

Leadership In Fatherhood

Fatherhood changed my understanding of leadership forever.

Before becoming a father, leadership felt personal.

After becoming a father, leadership became legacy.

Everything changed.

Because suddenly there was a little boy watching everything.

A little boy learning what manhood looked like.

A little boy learning what relationships looked like.

A little boy learning what courage looked like.

A little boy learning what integrity looked like.

And one day, that little boy will become a man.

The question is:

What kind of man?

Every father answers that question daily.

Not through words.

Through example.

That's why fatherhood is one of the highest forms of leadership.

Because it forces you to become the person you're asking someone else to become.

Leadership And Integrity

At its core, leadership is integrity.

Not perfection.

Integrity.

Doing what you said you'd do.

Honouring your values.

Keeping your word.

Following through.

Standing by your principles.

Especially when it's inconvenient.

Anyone can have values when life is easy.

Character appears when life becomes difficult.

Integrity is what remains when excuses disappear.

And integrity creates trust.

Trust creates influence.

Influence creates leadership.

Not the other way around.

The Elevated Man

The Elevated Man understands that leadership is not a title.

It's a way of living.

He doesn't wait for permission.

He doesn't wait for certainty.

He doesn't wait for confidence.

He takes responsibility.

He leads himself.

He leads through example.

He tells the truth.

He keeps his word.

He honours his values.

He accepts ownership.

And because of that, people trust him.

Not because he demands respect.

Because he earns it.

The Elevated Man knows that masculinity is not measured by dominance.

It's measured by responsibility.

By courage.

By integrity.

By service.

By presence.

By leadership.

Most importantly, he understands that leadership begins at home.

In the conversations nobody sees.

In the promises nobody applauds.

In the moments nobody celebrates.

Because character is built in private long before it's recognised in public.

The Elevated Man Challenge

Answer the following questions honestly:

Where am I avoiding responsibility?

What excuses am I still holding onto?

What area of my life needs stronger leadership?

What example am I currently setting for my children?

What would change if I fully accepted responsibility for my future?

Now answer one final question:

If my son copied every habit, behaviour, belief, and attitude I demonstrate today, would I be proud of the man he becomes?

Sit with that question.

Really sit with it.

Because leadership isn't about controlling others.

It's about becoming someone worth following.

The Elevated Man understands this.

And once he does, something remarkable happens.

He stops asking:

"How do I get people to follow me?"

And starts asking:

"How do I become a man I would follow myself?"

That question changes everything.

Because the greatest leadership journey you'll ever take isn't leading a team.

Or a business.

Or a family.

It's leading yourself.

And when you master that, every other form of leadership becomes possible.

That is the work.

That is the mission.

That is The Elevated Man.

CHAPTER SIXTEEN

My Son Asked If His Brain Was Broken

The lesson that changed everything

There are moments in life that divide everything into before and after.

Moments that seem ordinary when they begin.

Then something happens.

A sentence.

A conversation.

A question.

And suddenly nothing looks the same again.

This chapter is about one of those moments.

A moment that changed me forever.

A moment that ultimately became one of the reasons this book exists.

It started with a question.

A simple question.

The kind of question only a child can ask.

The kind of question that goes straight past your defences and directly into your heart.

"Daddy, do you think my brain is broken?"

I can still hear it.

I can still feel it.

And if I'm honest, part of me will probably hear it for the rest of my life.

The Question Behind The Question

At the time, Marinko was trying to make sense of his world.

Trying to understand why certain things felt harder for him than they seemed for other kids.

Trying to understand why his brain worked differently.

Why some days felt overwhelming.

Why emotions could feel bigger.

Why focus could be difficult.

Why he sometimes felt different.

As a father, there are moments when you desperately want to protect your child from pain.

This was one of those moments.

Because I knew he wasn't really asking about his brain.

Not entirely.

He was asking something deeper.

Something every human being asks at some point in their life.

Am I okay?

Am I normal?

Am I enough?

Do I belong?

Am I broken?

The words were different.

The question was universal.

The Punch In The Chest

I've been through difficult things in my life.

Depression.

Anxiety.

Identity crises.

Relationship struggles.

Work challenges.

Moments where life felt unbearably heavy.
Yet that question hit me harder than almost anything.
Because in that moment I wasn't looking at a diagnosis.
I wasn't looking at labels.
I wasn't looking at psychology.
I was looking at my son.
My beautiful little boy.
The boy who makes me laugh.
The boy who sees the world differently.
The boy who notices things others miss.
The boy whose heart is bigger than he realises.
The boy I would give my life for without hesitation.

And somehow that little boy had begun wondering if there was something wrong with him.

That thought broke me.
Because I knew exactly what it felt like.

The Secret Most Men Carry

The older I get, the more convinced I become that most men are carrying the same secret.

They simply hide it behind different masks.
Success.
Confidence.
Humour.
Work.
Achievement.
Relationships.
Status.
Strength.
Underneath all those masks is often the same question.
Am I enough?

Many men never say it out loud.

But they live it every day.

They chase success trying to answer it.

They chase approval trying to answer it.

They chase relationships trying to answer it.

They chase achievement trying to answer it.

They chase money trying to answer it.

They spend decades trying to answer a question that should never have existed in the first place.

I know because I did exactly that.

For years.

The Mirror

As Marinko stood there waiting for my answer, I realised something.

The question he was asking himself was the same question I'd spent most of my life asking.

Not:

Is my brain broken?

But:

Am I broken?

Am I enough?

Am I worthy?

Do I belong?

The details were different.

The wound was the same.

And suddenly I understood something profound.

The answer I gave him had to become the answer I gave myself.

Because children have an incredible ability to expose truths adults spend years avoiding.

What I Told Him

I looked at him and said:

"No mate. Your brain isn't broken."

Simple.

Direct.

True.

Then I explained something I'd spent years learning myself.

Different doesn't mean broken.

Different simply means different.

Some people are tall.

Some are short.

Some are naturally athletic.

Some are artistic.

Some are analytical.

Some are creative.

Some brains operate one way.

Some operate another.

None of that determines worth.

Worth isn't something you earn.

Worth isn't something you prove.

Worth isn't something you achieve.

Worth exists before all of those things.

I wanted him to understand that.

Not intellectually.

Deep in his bones.

Because life would eventually challenge him.

People would judge him.

Compare him.

Misunderstand him.

The world has a way of doing that.

I wanted him anchored in something stronger than public opinion.

I wanted him anchored in his own worth.

The Real Legacy

When I was younger, I thought legacy meant achievements.

Success.

Money.

Accomplishments.

Recognition.

Now I think differently.

Legacy is what you leave inside people.

Not what you leave behind.

The greatest legacy I will ever create isn't a business.

It isn't a book.

It isn't an achievement.

It's the beliefs my son carries into adulthood.

It's the way he sees himself.

It's the relationship he develops with his own mind.

It's the standards he adopts.

It's the courage he develops.

It's the love he experiences.

Because one day I'll be gone.

And when that day comes, I want him to carry something valuable.

Not my success.

My wisdom.

Not my achievements.

My beliefs.

Not my possessions.

My example.

That's legacy.

The Responsibility Of Fatherhood

Fatherhood is one of the most beautiful responsibilities a man can experience.

It's also one of the most confronting.

Because children don't just inherit our strengths.

They often inherit our unresolved wounds.

The beliefs we don't challenge.

The fears we don't confront.

The patterns we don't break.

The stories we continue telling ourselves.

Those things tend to travel through generations.

Unless someone decides to stop them.

That's one of the reasons this journey became so important to me.

I wasn't just doing it for myself.

I was doing it for my son.

Because every belief I heal is one less burden he has to carry.

Every pattern I break creates freedom for him.

Every lesson I learn becomes part of his inheritance.

Not financial inheritance.

Something far more valuable.

Emotional inheritance.

The Conversation Every Man Needs

If I'm honest, I think every man needs to have this conversation.

Maybe not with a child.

Maybe with himself.

Because deep down many men are still carrying an invisible version of that same question.

Am I broken?

Am I enough?

Do I matter?

Do I belong?

We've spent an entire book exploring different versions of that question.

The Nice Guy asks it through approval.

The people-pleaser asks it through sacrifice.

The perfectionist asks it through achievement.

The workaholic asks it through productivity.

The insecure man asks it through validation.

Different strategies.

Same question.

And every one of them leads to the same truth.

You were never broken.

The Day Everything Connected

As I reflected on that conversation later, something remarkable happened.

Every lesson I'd learned over the years suddenly connected.

The Alpha Code.

The personal development.

The therapy.

The mistakes.

The failures.

The depression.

The marriage struggles.

The identity work.

The emotional growth.

The leadership lessons.

Everything pointed toward one simple truth.

The transformation was never about becoming enough.

It was about realising I already was.

The Elevated Man is not a man who has fixed himself.

The Elevated Man is a man who has stopped believing he was broken.

That distinction changes everything.

What I Hope Marinko Learns

I don't need my son to become perfect.

I don't need him to become famous.

I don't need him to become wealthy.

I don't need him to become extraordinary.

I simply want him to know who he is.

To trust himself.

To value himself.

To respect himself.

To love himself.

To live courageously.

To tell the truth.

To honour his values.

To lead himself.

To understand that his worth was never up for debate.

If he learns those things, he'll be okay.

More than okay.

He'll be free.

The Elevated Man

The Elevated Man understands that every human being carries invisible wounds.

Invisible fears.

Invisible doubts.

Invisible questions.

He understands this because he's confronted his own.

And because he's confronted them, he no longer projects them onto others.

He no longer seeks external validation to soothe internal uncertainty.

He no longer spends his life proving himself.

He knows who he is.

He knows what he stands for.

He knows what he values.

Most importantly, he knows his worth.

Not because life guaranteed it.

Because he finally recognised it.

The Elevated Man Challenge

Imagine your son.

Or your daughter.

Or a young version of yourself.

Standing in front of you.

Looking up at you.

And asking:

"Do you think I'm broken?"

What would you say?

Write down your answer.

Every word.

Every sentence.

Every belief.

Now read it back.

Slowly.

Because whatever answer you would give that child is probably the answer you need to give yourself.

Most men spend their lives searching for evidence that they're enough.

The Elevated Man eventually discovers something different.

He always was.

The proof was never required.

Only the belief.

And perhaps that's the lesson I hope my son carries long after I'm gone.

Not that life will be easy.

Not that he won't struggle.

Not that he won't fail.

But that no matter what happens...

No matter how different he feels.

No matter what challenges he faces.

No matter what the world says.

He was never broken.

And neither are you.

CHAPTER SEVENTEEN

Built For More

The man waiting beneath the conditioning

At some point during every man's journey, he encounters a question that changes everything.

Not:

What do I want?

Not:

How much money do I want to make?

Not:

How successful do I want to become?

The question is deeper.

More uncomfortable.

More important.

It sounds like this:

Why am I here?

Not in some philosophical, sit-on-a-mountain-and-stare-at-the-sunset kind of way.

I mean genuinely.

Why are you here?

What are you building?

What are you contributing?

What kind of life are you creating?

What kind of man are you becoming?

And perhaps most importantly:

What happens if you never answer those questions?

Because here's what I've learned.

A man can survive without certainty.

A man can survive hardship.

A man can survive failure.

A man can survive enormous amounts of pain.

But a man who loses his sense of purpose slowly begins losing himself.

The Day Success Stopped Being Enough

One of the strangest experiences in life is discovering that achievement doesn't solve the problem you thought it would.

Most men spend years chasing goals.

Money.

Status.

Recognition.

Success.

Accomplishments.

And there is absolutely nothing wrong with those things.

The problem occurs when you expect them to provide meaning.

Because they can't.

Not permanently.

Success is wonderful.

But success without purpose eventually feels empty.

Achievement without meaning eventually feels hollow.

Winning a game you never wanted to play is still losing.

Many men discover this far too late.

They climb a ladder only to realise it's leaning against the wrong wall.

The Question That Haunted Me

After some of the darkest periods of my life, I found myself asking a question I had never seriously considered before.

What am I actually trying to do with my life?

Not next week.

Not next month.

Not next year.

My life.

Because for years my focus had been survival.

Pay the bills.

Look after the family.

Manage responsibilities.

Handle problems.

Get through another day.

Again, those things matter.

But survival and purpose are not the same thing.

One keeps you alive.

The other makes life worth living.

And eventually every man must decide whether he's merely surviving or actually living.

You Were Built For More

The title of this book didn't come from motivation.

It came from observation.

I've spent years watching men.

Listening to them.

Coaching them.

Learning from them.

And I keep noticing the same thing.

Most men dramatically underestimate themselves.

Not their talent.

Not their intelligence.

Their potential.

Because somewhere along the way they accepted a smaller version of themselves.

A safer version.

A more comfortable version.

A more socially acceptable version.

They stopped dreaming.

Stopped growing.

Stopped challenging themselves.

Stopped believing they were capable of more.

Not because they lacked potential.

Because life convinced them to shrink.

Responsibilities.

Failures.

Fear.

Disappointments.

Criticism.

Rejection.

The weight of life slowly compressed their vision.

And eventually they forgot who they were capable of becoming.

This book exists to remind you.

You were built for more.

Not more status.

Not more possessions.

More truth.

More courage.

More purpose.

More impact.

More leadership.

More life.

The Difference Between Existing And Living

Have you ever met someone who was technically alive but not really living?

Maybe you've been that person.

I know I have.

Wake up.

Go to work.

Come home.

Watch television.

Go to sleep.

Repeat.

Day after day.

Month after month.

Year after year.

Life becomes routine.

Predictable.

Comfortable.

And quietly empty.

Nothing is dramatically wrong.

Yet something feels missing.

That feeling isn't weakness.

It's your soul demanding more.

Your spirit reminding you that you weren't designed merely to exist.

You were designed to contribute.

To create.

To grow.

To love.

To lead.

To serve.

To become.

The discomfort isn't the problem.

The discomfort is the invitation.

The Mission Gap

One thing I've noticed about men is that we function differently when we have a mission.

Not a goal.

A mission.

Goals are temporary.

Missions transform identity.

A goal says:

"I want to lose weight."

A mission says:

"I want to become a man who leads himself."

A goal says:

"I want more money."

A mission says:

"I want to create freedom for my family."

A goal says:

"I want a better marriage."

A mission says:

"I want to become the kind of husband my wife deserves."

Goals end.

Missions evolve.

And mission creates meaning.

Meaning creates resilience.

Resilience creates strength.

That's why purpose matters.

Because purpose gives suffering somewhere to go.

The Men Who Changed My Life

Throughout my journey, I've been fortunate enough to learn from extraordinary men.

Leon Wilken, Lucas Cope, Clay Greenbank, Justin Dulihanty and Kalan Hall.

Men who challenged me.

Supported me.

Confronted me.

Believed in me.

Men who refused to let me stay small.

One thing they all had in common was this:

They were living intentionally.

Not perfectly.

Intentionally.

They had standards.

Vision.

Purpose.

Direction.

They understood that masculinity isn't something you inherit.

It's something you cultivate.

Day by day.

Decision by decision.

Choice by choice.

Watching those men taught me something powerful.

Growth is contagious.

When one man rises, others rise with him.

And that's exactly why this mission matters.

The Ripple Effect

Most men underestimate the impact they have.

You matter more than you think.

Your attitude matters.

Your example matters.

Your courage matters.

Your integrity matters.

Your growth matters.

Your healing matters.

Your children are watching.

Your wife is watching.

Your friends are watching.

Your community is watching.

You don't get to decide whether you're influencing people.

You already are.

The only question is:

What are you teaching them?

Every man creates ripples.

The Elevated Man creates ripples worth following.

What More Actually Means

When I say you were built for more, I don't mean you need a bigger house.

A bigger bank account.

A bigger business.

A bigger audience.

Maybe you'll have those things.

Maybe you won't.

That's not the point.

More means becoming more fully yourself.

More courageous.

More honest.

More disciplined.

More present.

More loving.

More authentic.

More purposeful.

More aligned.

More alive.

Because the greatest tragedy isn't failing.

The greatest tragedy is dying with your potential still trapped inside you.

The Elevated Man

The Elevated Man understands that life is not about comfort.

It's about contribution.

He understands that purpose is not found.

It's built.

Created.

Earned through action.

He understands that his mission is larger than himself.

His family.

His community.

His legacy.

The future generations he influences.

He knows that every day presents a choice.

Shrink.

Or expand.

Hide.

Or lead.

Exist.

Or live.

And because he understands that choice, he takes responsibility for his life.

Not perfectly.

Consistently.

That's enough.

The Elevated Man Challenge

Imagine it's your 80th birthday.

The people you love most have gathered to celebrate your life.

Your wife.

Your children.

Your grandchildren.

Your friends.

Former colleagues.

People whose lives you touched.

One by one they stand and describe the man you became.

What do you want them to say?

Write it down.

Every word.

Every quality.

Every characteristic.

Every value.

Now ask yourself:

Am I living in a way that makes that future possible?

If not, what needs to change?

What conversation needs to happen?

What decision needs to be made?

What fear needs to be faced?

What action needs to be taken?

Then do it.

Because life moves quickly.

Faster than you think.

And one day the story of your life will be complete.

The question is not whether that day will come.

The question is what story will be told when it does.

You were not born to drift.

You were not born to settle.

You were not born to live someone else's life.

You were built for more.

The only question left is:

What are you going to do about it?

CHAPTER EIGHTEN

The Legacy You Leave

What remains after you're gone

Most men think legacy is something you leave behind when you die.

I used to think that too.

A business.

A house.

Money.

Investments.

Achievements.

Awards.

A name on a plaque somewhere.

The older I get, the more I realise how wrong that is.

Legacy isn't what you leave behind.

Legacy is what you leave inside people.

And whether you realise it or not, you're building your legacy right now.

Today.

In this moment.

Not someday.

Now.

The Funeral Exercise

Let's do something uncomfortable.

Imagine your funeral.

I know.

Not exactly the uplifting start you were hoping for.

Stick with me.

Imagine the room is full.

Your wife is there.

Your children.

Your grandchildren.

Your closest mates.

People you've worked with.

People you've helped.

People you've loved.

One by one they stand up and tell stories about your life.

What do they say?

Not what do you hope they say.

What would they actually say if the funeral was tomorrow?

That's a different question.

A much more honest question.

Because legacy isn't built through intentions.

It's built through actions.

Not what you meant to do.

What you actually did.

Not who you wanted to become.

Who you became.

That's why this exercise matters.

Because most men spend their lives planning a future they'll never create.

The Elevated Man starts living it now.

The Inheritance Nobody Talks About

When most people think about inheritance, they think about money.

Assets.

Property.

Wealth.

And there's nothing wrong with that.

Providing for your family matters.

But I've learned something through fatherhood.

The most valuable inheritance you'll ever give your children is not financial.

It's psychological.

Emotional.

Spiritual.

It's the beliefs you pass down.

The standards you model.

The values you live.

The example you set.

Children inherit far more than eye colour and genetics.

They inherit stories.

Beliefs.

Patterns.

Habits.

Mindsets.

Fears.

Confidence.

Shame.

Courage.

Integrity.

Whether we like it or not, we become teachers.

The question is:

What are we teaching?

The Generational Relay Race

I want you to imagine life as a relay race.

Every generation receives a baton.

Some parts of that baton are beautiful.

Love.

Strength.

Work ethic.

Resilience.

Family values.

Traditions.

Wisdom.

Some parts aren't.

Fear.

Shame.

Trauma.

Silence.

People-pleasing.

Emotional suppression.

Self-doubt.

Every generation has a choice.

Pass the baton unchanged.

Or improve it before handing it forward.

That's what this journey has been for me.

Not perfection.

Improvement.

Taking what was useful.

Healing what wasn't.

Then handing something better to Marinko.

That's legacy.

Not perfection.

Progress.

The Man My Son Sees

One of the questions I ask myself regularly is:

What kind of man does my son see?

Not what kind of man do I think I am.

What kind of man does he actually see?

Does he see a man who keeps his word?

Does he see a man who tells the truth?

Does he see a man who respects his wife?

Does he see a man who leads himself?

Does he see a man who apologises when he's wrong?

Does he see a man who has courage?

Does he see a man who lives with integrity?

Because children don't learn from our advice.

They learn from our example.

You can tell your child to be confident.

But if you constantly doubt yourself, they'll learn self-doubt.

You can tell your child to set boundaries.

But if you constantly abandon yourself, they'll learn self-abandonment.

You can tell your child to be courageous.

But if fear runs your life, they'll learn fear.

Leadership starts at home.

Legacy starts at home.

Everything starts at home.

The Things Nobody Will Remember

Here's a truth that hit me hard.

One day nobody will care how many emails you answered.

Nobody will care how many meetings you attended.

Nobody will care about most of the things that currently consume your attention.

The world will move on.

That's not depressing.

It's freeing.

Because it helps clarify what actually matters.

People won't remember your workload.

They'll remember your presence.

They won't remember your job title.

They'll remember how you made them feel.

They won't remember your excuses.

They'll remember your character.

Character survives.

Everything else fades.

The Quiet Legacy

Most meaningful legacies are invisible.

A conversation.

A lesson.

A moment of encouragement.

A boundary.

An apology.

A hug.

A difficult truth.

A moment of courage.

A moment of love.

The world celebrates grand gestures.

Life is usually changed by small ones.

The advice your father gave you.

The teacher who believed in you.

The friend who showed up when nobody else did.

The stranger who said exactly what you needed to hear.

Those moments matter.

And you'll create more of them than you realise.

That's why your life matters.

Even when it feels ordinary.

Especially when it feels ordinary.

The Legacy Of The Nice Guy

Many Nice Guys leave behind a confusing legacy.

People describe them as:

Helpful.

Generous.

Reliable.

Kind.

But beneath those compliments often sits another truth.

They weren't fully known.

They spent so much time managing other people's perceptions that nobody truly knew them.

Not even themselves.

That's a tragedy.

Because being liked is not the same as being known.

And being known is one of the deepest human needs.

I don't want people standing at my funeral saying:

"He made everyone happy."

I want them saying:

"He was real."

"He was honest."

"He was courageous."

"He lived according to his values."

"He loved deeply."

"He became himself."

That's a legacy worth pursuing.

The Ripple Effect

Think about every person whose life you've influenced.

Family.

Friends.

Children.

Partners.

Colleagues.

Neighbours.

Strangers.

Now think about the people they've influenced.

And the people those people influenced.

The ripple effect becomes impossible to measure.

One act of courage can echo through generations.

One act of healing can change an entire family tree.

One decision to break a destructive pattern can alter the future for people you'll never meet.

That's why your growth matters.

Not just for you.

For everyone connected to you.

The impact is far greater than you realise.

The Real Measure Of A Man

For years I measured success through achievement.

Many men do.

Income.

Results.

Progress.

Accomplishments.

Now I measure success differently.

Did I tell the truth?

Did I honour my values?

Did I keep my word?

Did I love my family well?

Did I show up fully?

Did I become more of who I was capable of becoming?

That's the scoreboard now.

And strangely enough, life became much more meaningful when I changed the way I kept score.

The Elevated Man

The Elevated Man understands that legacy is not built at the end of life.

It's built every day.

Through choices.

Habits.

Standards.

Conversations.

Relationships.

Actions.

He understands that every day he is teaching people how to live.

Whether he intends to or not.

So he chooses carefully.

He lives intentionally.

He heals what he can.

He strengthens what he can.

He leaves people better than he found them.

Not because he's perfect.

Because he cares.

Because he understands that the greatest legacy a man can leave is not evidence of his success.

It's evidence of his character.

The Elevated Man Challenge

Take out a notebook and complete the following exercise.

Write your own eulogy.

Not the version you'd like people to read.

The version you want to earn.

Describe:

The husband you became.

The father you became.

The leader you became.

The friend you became.

The man you became.

Then ask yourself:

What habits would that man practice daily?

What standards would he refuse to compromise?

What fears would he need to overcome?

What actions would he take today?

Because legacy is not built tomorrow.

It's built today.

In ordinary moments.

Ordinary conversations.

Ordinary decisions.

One choice at a time.

And one day, long after you're gone, the quality of those choices will become your story.

The question is: What story are you writing?

Because whether you realise it or not...

The next chapter of that story begins the moment you turn this page.

CHAPTER NINETEEN

The Elevated Man Code

Twelve principles for a life of meaning

Every man lives by a code.

Whether he realises it or not.

Some men consciously choose theirs.

Most inherit one by accident.

From parents.

Culture.

Friends.

Fear.

Past experiences.

Social conditioning.

The result is that many men spend their lives operating under beliefs they never intentionally selected.

Rules they never examined.

Standards they never questioned.

Expectations they never agreed to.

And then they wonder why they feel disconnected.

Why life feels misaligned.

Why success feels empty.

Why relationships feel difficult.

Why something feels off.

The answer is simple.

You cannot build an extraordinary life using someone else's blueprint.

Eventually every man must decide what he stands for.

This chapter is my answer.

Not because it's perfect.

Not because it's complete.

Because it's the code that helped save my life.

The code that rebuilt my marriage.

The code that transformed my relationship with myself.

The code that became the foundation of The Elevated Man.

Take what serves you.

Challenge what doesn't.

Then create your own.

But whatever you do...

Live by something.

Because drifting is not a strategy.

Principle One:

Tell The Truth

Everything begins here.

Not with confidence.

Not with discipline.

Not with success.

Truth.

The truth about your life.

The truth about your behaviour.

The truth about your fears.

The truth about your relationships.

The truth about your excuses.

The truth about your desires.

The truth about your standards.

Without truth, transformation is impossible.

You cannot change what you refuse to acknowledge.

Most men don't need more information.

They need more honesty.

The Elevated Man tells the truth.

Especially when it's uncomfortable.

Especially when it costs him.

Principle Two:

Take Responsibility

The moment you stop blaming is the moment your life changes.

Not because life is always fair.

Because responsibility creates power.

Victims wait.

Leaders act.

The Elevated Man accepts responsibility for:

His actions.

His decisions.

His mindset.

His emotions.

His future.

He may not be responsible for everything that happened.

But he is responsible for what happens next.

Always.

Principle Three:

Keep Your Word

Nothing destroys self-respect faster than breaking promises to yourself.

Nothing.

Every time you say you'll do something and don't, self-trust weakens.

Every time you follow through, self-trust strengthens.

Confidence is not built through positive thinking.

Confidence is built through evidence.

Evidence that you can trust yourself.

The Elevated Man does what he says he'll do.

Not perfectly.

Consistently.

Principle Four:

Choose Courage Over Comfort

Fear never disappears.

Read that again.

Fear never disappears.

Waiting for fear to leave is like waiting for the ocean to stop producing waves.

It's not happening.

The question isn't:

Am I afraid?

The question is:

What does courage require?

The Elevated Man understands that growth lives on the other side of discomfort.

So he acts anyway.

Principle Five:

Love Without Losing Yourself

Love is one of the most beautiful experiences available to us.

It's also one of the easiest places to lose ourselves.

The Elevated Man loves deeply.

But he remains connected to himself.

He does not sacrifice his identity for approval.

He does not abandon his values for harmony.

He does not trade authenticity for acceptance.

He understands that healthy love requires two whole people.

Not two people disappearing into each other.

Principle Six:

Set Boundaries Without Guilt

A boundary is simply self-respect made visible.

The Elevated Man understands that saying no is not selfish.

Honouring his values is not selfish.

Protecting his time is not selfish.

Protecting his energy is not selfish.

Protecting his peace is not selfish.

He understands that every meaningful thing in life requires protection.

Including himself.

Principle Seven:

Feel Everything Be Ruled By Nothing

The Elevated Man does not fear emotions.

He does not suppress them.

He does not worship them.

He understands them.

Processes them.

Learns from them.

Uses them.

Fear gets information.

Anger gets information.

Sadness gets information.

But none of them get control.

That's emotional mastery.

Principle Eight:

Become The Man You Needed

This principle changed my life.

Many men spend years wishing someone had saved them.

Guided them.

Supported them.

Believed in them.

Protected them.

The Elevated Man stops waiting.

He becomes that man.

For himself.

For his family.

For his children.

For others.

He becomes the example he once needed.

Principle Nine:

Lead Yourself First

Leadership starts in private.

Not public.

Not on social media.

Not in boardrooms.

Not in speeches.

Private.

In habits.

In discipline.

In standards.

In integrity.

In self-control.

If you cannot lead yourself, eventually life will lead you.

Usually somewhere you don't want to go.

The Elevated Man leads himself first.

Everything else grows from there.

Principle Ten:

Leave People Better Than You Found Them

This is one of the simplest principles in the entire code.

And one of the most powerful.

Leave people better than you found them.

Not because you're trying to save them.

Because you care.

Offer encouragement.

Offer honesty.

Offer support.

Offer leadership.

Offer kindness.

Offer strength.

The world has enough critics.

Become a builder.

Principle Eleven:

Protect What Matters

Not everything deserves equal attention.

Not everything deserves equal energy.

The Elevated Man understands priorities.

His family.

His health.

His integrity.

His values.

His mission.

His relationships.

These things matter.

He protects them accordingly.

Because what you fail to protect eventually disappears.

Principle Twelve:

Never Stop Becoming

One of the greatest mistakes a man can make is believing he's finished.

Finished learning.

Finished growing.

Finished evolving.

Life has a way of humbling that belief quickly.

The Elevated Man remains a student.

Always.

Curious.

Open.

Growth-oriented.

Committed.

He understands that becoming is a lifelong process.

Not a destination.

The Code In Action

A code is useless if it only exists on paper.

Anybody can agree with principles.

The challenge is living them.

When you're tired.

When you're stressed.

When you're afraid.

When you're angry.

When you're hurt.

When life gets messy.

That's where character appears.

Not in perfect conditions.

In difficult ones.

Anybody can lead when life is easy.

Character reveals itself when life becomes difficult.

That's why standards matter.

That's why values matter.

That's why codes matter.

Because in moments of uncertainty, they provide direction.

The Promise

When I first began this journey, I thought I needed confidence.

Then I thought I needed discipline.

Then I thought I needed success.

Then I thought I needed approval.

Then I thought I needed certainty.

I was wrong.

What I needed was a code.

Something stronger than emotions.

Stronger than circumstances.

Stronger than fear.

A set of principles capable of guiding me when life became difficult.

This code became that foundation.

And perhaps it can become part of yours.

The Elevated Man Challenge

Create your own code.

Not tomorrow.

Today.

Ten principles.

Ten standards.

Ten commitments.

Simple.

Clear.

Non-negotiable.

Then write them somewhere visible.

Read them daily.

Live them relentlessly.

Not because perfection is possible.

Because direction is.

Because identity is built through repetition.

Because character is built through action.

Because every great man lives by a code.

And because the quality of your life will ultimately be determined by the quality of the principles you refuse to compromise.

The Elevated Man is not defined by his circumstances.

His income.

His status.

His achievements.

His past.

His mistakes.

He is defined by the standards he chooses to live by.

And those standards become his legacy.

This is my code.

Now it's time to write yours.

CHAPTER TWENTY

The Man In The Mirror

Coming home to yourself

If you've made it this far, I want to ask you a question.

A simple question.

One that may be more important than anything else we've discussed in this book.

When you look in the mirror now...

Who do you see?

Not your job.

Not your title.

Not your achievements.

Not your failures.

Not the masks.

Not the roles.

You.

Who do you see?

Because twenty chapters ago, we began with a man who had forgotten who he was.

A man who measured his worth through approval.

A man who confused being needed with being loved.

A man who abandoned himself to keep the peace.

A man who believed his value had to be earned.

A man who spent years performing.

Proving.

Pleasing.

Pretending.

And maybe, if you're honest, parts of that man felt familiar.

Maybe they still do.

That's okay.

Transformation isn't about becoming perfect.

It's about becoming conscious.

And if you've come this far, you're already more conscious than you were when we began.

The Man I Used To Be

I want to tell you something.

The man who attempted to end his life is still part of me.

The man who doubted himself.

The man who sought approval.

The man who feared rejection.

The man who felt lost.

The man who felt broken.

He's still there.

The difference is that he no longer drives the car.

For years I thought growth meant eliminating weakness.

Eliminating fear.

Eliminating insecurity.

Eliminating doubt.

I was wrong.

Growth isn't about eliminating parts of yourself.

It's about learning which parts deserve the steering wheel.

Fear still speaks.

Doubt still speaks.

Insecurity still speaks.

The difference is that I no longer mistake them for truth.

And neither should you.

The Mirror Never Lies

One of the reasons I called this chapter The Man In The Mirror is because mirrors are brutally honest.

They don't care about excuses.

They don't care about intentions.

They don't care about who you want to be.

They simply reflect who you are.

Most men spend years avoiding mirrors.

Not physical mirrors.

Psychological mirrors.

Truth.

Feedback.

Reflection.

Accountability.

Because those things are uncomfortable.

But discomfort is where growth lives.

Every breakthrough I've ever experienced began with a mirror.

A moment where I stopped blaming.

Stopped avoiding.

Stopped performing.

And finally looked at myself honestly.

Not with judgement.

With responsibility.

That's where transformation begins.

Not when you learn something new.

When you tell yourself the truth.

You Were Never Broken

If there is one message I hope survives long after you've forgotten my name, it's this:

You were never broken.

Wounded?

Maybe.

Conditioned?

Absolutely.

Lost?

Possibly.

Scared?

Probably.

But broken?

No.

The world has a way of convincing men they're not enough.

Not successful enough.

Not strong enough.

Not confident enough.

Not attractive enough.

Not wealthy enough.

Not masculine enough.

Not worthy enough.

Then it sells them solutions to problems that never existed.

The greatest lie many men believe is that worthiness is something to achieve.

It isn't.

It's something to recognise.

You do not become worthy.

You are worthy.

Growth simply helps you express it.

That distinction changed my life.

I hope it changes yours.

The Real Meaning Of The Elevated Man

When I first started this journey, I thought becoming an Elevated Man meant becoming stronger.

More confident.

More disciplined.

More successful.

More respected.

Now I understand something different.

The Elevated Man is not a destination.

He's a commitment.

A commitment to truth.

A commitment to growth.

A commitment to courage.

A commitment to responsibility.

A commitment to integrity.

A commitment to becoming more fully yourself.

Every day.

Not perfectly.

Consistently.

The Elevated Man still struggles.

Still fails.

Still makes mistakes.

Still gets scared.

Still gets things wrong.

The difference is that he no longer runs from those realities.

He faces them.

Learns from them.

Grows through them.

That's what elevates him.

Not perfection.

Ownership.

The Gift Jana Gave Me

When I think about my life, there are many moments I'm grateful for.

Meeting Jana.

Marrying Jana.

Building a life together.

Travelling the world together.

Raising our son together.

Those memories mean everything to me.

But perhaps the greatest gift she ever gave me wasn't love.

It was reflection.

Because relationships have a way of showing us who we really are.

Not who we pretend to be.

Not who we'd like to be.

Who we actually are.

And through the challenges, the growth, the mistakes, and the lessons, I eventually realised something.

The strongest version of myself wasn't created.

It was uncovered.

Buried underneath fear.

Approval.

Conditioning.

Self-doubt.

People-pleasing.

Waiting patiently for me to find him again.

Maybe that's true for you too.

The Gift Marinko Gave Me

And then there is my son.

The little boy who asked if his brain was broken.

The little boy who unknowingly became one of my greatest teachers.

Because every lesson I wanted him to learn forced me to learn it first.

Every piece of wisdom I wanted to pass on required me to embody it.

Every standard I wanted him to live by challenged me to live by it myself.

Children have a way of doing that.

They don't ask us to be perfect.

They ask us to be authentic.

And because of him, I became far more committed to becoming the man I wanted him to see.

Not the man I wanted the world to see.

The man I wanted my son to see.

That's a very different thing.

The Invitation

Now I want to invite you to do something.

Not tomorrow.

Not next week.

Today.

I want you to stop waiting.

Stop waiting for confidence.

Stop waiting for certainty.

Stop waiting for motivation.

Stop waiting for permission.

Stop waiting for the perfect moment.

The perfect moment does not exist.

The perfect version of you does not exist.

Life is happening now.

Your future is being created now.

Your legacy is being created now.

The man you're becoming is being shaped now.

Not when you're ready.

Now.

The Question

Before we finish, I want to leave you with one final question.

Imagine you're standing in front of a mirror.

Not a physical mirror.

A mirror that reflects your character.

Your integrity.

Your courage.

Your honesty.

Your standards.

Your choices.

The real you.

Not the image.

Not the performance.

The truth.

You look into that mirror and ask:

"Am I becoming the man I am capable of becoming?"

What answer comes back?

Don't rush it.

Sit with it.

Because that question matters more than your income.

More than your status.

More than your achievements.

More than anyone else's opinion.

Because at the end of your life, that's the question that will remain.

Not:

Did everyone like me?

Not:

Did I avoid failure?

Not:

Did I stay comfortable?

But:

Did I become who I was capable of becoming?

My Promise To You

I cannot promise that life will become easier. It won't.

Life remains life.

Challenges will come.

Pain will come.

Loss will come.

Fear will come.

Uncertainty will come.

That's part of the deal.

But I can promise you this. The man who walks through those challenges with self-respect, courage, integrity, and purpose experiences life differently. Because he is different.

Not superior.

Different.

Grounded.

Aligned.

Authentic.

Free.

And freedom changes everything.

EPILOGUE

The Beginning

If you're reading this, you've reached the end of the book.

Congratulations.

Seriously.

Not because finishing a book is difficult.

Because if you've read every chapter, you've done something many men spend their entire lives avoiding.

You've looked at yourself honestly.

You've questioned your beliefs.

You've confronted uncomfortable truths.

You've examined your fears.

You've challenged your excuses.

You've taken responsibility.

And that takes courage.

More courage than most people realise.

But before you celebrate reaching the final page, I need to tell you something important.

This is not the end.

It's the beginning.

The Trap

One of the biggest traps in personal development is believing that knowledge creates transformation.

It doesn't.

Knowledge creates awareness.

Action creates transformation.

I've met men who can quote every self-help book ever written.

They can explain psychology.

Stoicism.

Masculinity.

Relationships.

Mindset.

Purpose.

Leadership.

Yet their lives never change.

Why?

Because understanding something and living something are two very different things.

Reading about courage is not courage.

Reading about boundaries is not boundaries.

Reading about leadership is not leadership.

Reading about transformation is not transformation.

The work begins when the book closes.

Not while it's open.

What Happens Next

Here's what's probably going to happen.

You're going to feel motivated.

Inspired.

Clear.

Determined.

You'll make some decisions.

Set some standards.

Commit to change.

Then life will happen.

You'll get busy.

You'll get tired.

You'll get distracted.

Old habits will return.

Old fears will resurface.

Old patterns will reappear.

You'll people-please again.

You'll avoid a difficult conversation.

You'll break a promise to yourself.

You'll doubt yourself.

You'll question whether you've actually changed.

And when that happens, I want you to remember something.

That is not failure.

That is being human.

Growth is not a straight line.

It never was.

It never will be.

The Elevated Man is not the man who never falls.

He's the man who keeps getting back up.

The Myth Of Arrival

For years I thought there would be a moment when I finally arrived.

A moment when I'd feel confident all the time.

Certain all the time.

Strong all the time.

Happy all the time.

At peace all the time.

I kept chasing that moment.

It never came.

And that's good news.

Because life isn't about arriving.

It's about becoming.

The day you believe you've arrived is the day growth ends.

The Elevated Man remains a student.

Always.

Learning.

Adjusting.

Growing.

Refining.

Becoming.

There is no finish line.

Only the next step.

The Promise You Made

Somewhere throughout this book, whether you realised it or not, you made a promise.

Not to me.

To yourself.

You promised yourself that things would be different.

That you would stop settling.

Stop hiding.

Stop performing.

Stop abandoning yourself.

Stop living beneath your potential.

That promise matters.

Protect it.

Because your future will be shaped less by motivation and more by the promises you keep.

Especially the promises nobody else knows about.

The Men Who Come After You

One day someone will benefit from the work you're doing right now.

Maybe your son.

Maybe your daughter.

Maybe your wife.

Maybe your future partner.

Maybe a friend.

Maybe a colleague.

Maybe someone you've never met.

They'll benefit because you chose to heal.

Because you chose to grow.

Because you chose to tell the truth.

Because you chose courage over comfort.

They may never know the battles you fought internally.

The fears you confronted.

The nights you struggled.

The habits you broke.

The beliefs you challenged.

But they'll experience the result.

And that matters.

More than you realise.

Every man who does this work changes more than himself.

He changes the people around him.

And often the generations that follow.

The Man In The Mirror

When you finish reading these words, I want you to do something.

Find a mirror.

Not tomorrow.

Today.

Stand in front of it.

Look yourself in the eyes.

And ask yourself:

Who am I becoming?

Not who was I.

Not who should I be.

Who am I becoming?

Then ask:

Am I proud of the direction I'm heading?

Not perfection.

Direction.

Because direction determines destiny.

And every day you are either moving toward the man you want to become or away from him.

The choice is yours.

It always has been.

My Final Message

If there is one thing I hope you take from this book, it's this:

You do not need to earn your worth.

You do not need to prove your value.

You do not need permission to become yourself.

You do not need to wait until you're ready.

You do not need to become someone else.

You simply need the courage to stop abandoning who you already are.

The world does not need another man pretending to be someone he's not.

The world needs more men willing to tell the truth.

More men willing to lead.

More men willing to take responsibility.

More men willing to love deeply.

More men willing to break destructive cycles.

More men willing to stand for something.

More men willing to become themselves.

That is The Elevated Man.

Not perfect.

Not fearless.

Not flawless.

Authentic.

Responsible.

Courageous.

Grounded.

Free.

One Last Thing

Twenty years ago, a young bloke sitting in his car saw a beautiful woman walking along the Mandurah Foreshore.

Terrified, he threw his phone number out the window and drove away.

He had no idea what was waiting for him.

No idea what challenges he would face.

No idea what lessons life would teach him.

No idea how many times he would lose himself.

Or find himself again.

No idea that one day he would write these words.

But looking back now, I can see something clearly.

Every challenge.

Every failure.

Every setback.

Every lesson.

Every breakthrough.

Every painful moment.

Every beautiful moment.

Led here.

To this.

To the understanding that changed everything.

You do not need to earn your worth.

You do not need to prove your value.

You do not need permission to become yourself.

You never did.

You were built for more.

Not because you're special.

Because you're human.

And inside every man is a version of himself waiting to emerge.

Stronger.

Wiser.

More courageous.

More authentic.

More alive.

The question has never been whether that man exists.

The question is whether you're willing to become him.

The mirror is waiting.

Go meet him.

Go become the man you've spent the last twenty chapters meeting.

He's been waiting for you all along.

Welcome home.

— Cade Brown

Built For More

The Elevated Man Project

ABOUT THE AUTHOR

Cade Brown is a husband, father, Brazilian Jiu-Jitsu Black Belt, student of life, and men's development advocate. For much of his life, Cade looked like he had it together. He was hardworking, dependable, family-oriented, and committed to being a good man.

Yet beneath the surface, he struggled with many of the same challenges faced by countless men today—people-pleasing, approval-seeking, self-doubt, poor boundaries, emotional suppression, and a deep disconnection from his own identity.

After reaching one of the lowest points of his life, Cade embarked on a journey of self-discovery and transformation that would fundamentally change how he saw himself, his relationships, and his purpose.

Through years of personal development, coaching, mentorship, the Men's Development Academy, and countless lessons learned through experience, Cade developed a new understanding of masculinity—one rooted not in dominance or performance, but in self-respect, responsibility, courage, emotional intelligence, and character.

Built For More was born from that journey.

Cade wrote this book to help men reconnect with themselves, break free from destructive patterns, and become the leaders, husbands, fathers, and men they were capable of becoming all along.

Cade is passionate about helping men develop stronger identities, healthier relationships, and a deeper sense of purpose. His mission is simple:

To help men stop living beneath their potential and start becoming the men they were built to be.

www.ingramcontent.com/pod-product-compliance
Lightning Source LLC
LaVergne TN
LVHW020233210926
848481LV00016B/1823